Praise for *Tiny Ladies in Shiny Pants*

"*Tiny Ladies* is a stand-out memoir from Jill Soloway about the friction of assimilation and rebellion—a Jewish girl who's raised "young, gifted, and black," a sorority pledger who's a take-no-prisoners feminist, and a celebrity groupie who searches for intimacy with the authentic and unprepossessing."
　　　—Susie Bright, editor of *Three Kinds of Asking for It*

"When Jill Soloway writes about sex, desire and politics, she does it in such an endearing, compelling and hilarious way that you not only want to listen, you must. *Tiny Ladies in Shiny Pants* is a profound delight."
　　　—Nancy Friday, author of *My Secret Garden*

"You wish Jill Soloway were at your dinner party to impress your friends with an avalanche of raw, wildly funny, uncensored observations and opinions that inevitably rally you to her cause."
　　　—Hillary Liftin, author of *Candy and Me*

"I'm such a fan of everything Jill writes, and this is no exception. Each chapter is a funny and poignant treat. She's not trying to preach, not trying to be *feminist of the moment*—she's just figuring out her life in the context of our world, and it transcends."
　　　—Sarah Silverman, comedienne, screenwriter, *Funny Ladies, Saturday Night Live*

*f*P

Tiny
Ladies
in
Shiny
Pants

Based on a True Story

◉

Jill Soloway

FREE PRESS

New York London Toronto Sydney

FREE PRESS
A Division of Simon & Schuster, Inc.
1230 Avenue of the Americas
New York, NY 10020

For information about special discounts for bulk purchases,
please contact Simon & Schuster Special Sales: 1-800-456-6798
or business@simonandschuster.com

Designed by Karolina Harris

Manufactured in the United States of America
10 9 8 7 6 5 4 3 2 1

Library of Congress Cataloging-in-Publication Data

Soloway, Jill.
Tiny Ladies in shiny pants / Jill Soloway.
p. cm.
1. Soloway, Jill. 2. Authors, American—21st century—Biography. 3. Television
producers and directors—United States—Biography. 4. Theatrical producers
and directors—United States—Biography. 5. Television writers—United
States—Biography. I. Title.

PS3619.0439T56 2005
813'.6—dc22
[B]   2005048714

ISBN-13: 978-0-7432-7217-9
ISBN-10:   0-7432-7217-X

For my family

Contents

Tiny
Ladies
in
Shiny
Pants

◉

Introduction A
or
The Porno-ization
of America

I'm done writing about sex.

If you bought this book because you thought there would be sex in it, get in your car, drive to your local bookstore, and throw it in the face of the cashier. You will find NO SEX here. None.

Something happened to me the other night that changed everything. I was at a restaurant with a bunch of people and my friend Sarah asked, "Have you guys heard about these rainbow parties?"

"What's a rainbow party?" I asked.

"Rainbow parties are these things fourteen-year-olds are doing."

"Oh, like a sleepover where for dessert you make Jell-O in different colors and stack it up with Cool Whip on top? Called a rainbow parfait, right?"

"Noooooo," she answered.

"Oh, I know," I offered. "We had them when we were little, my mom would be doing one of her activist mailings for the Rainbow Coalition? And we would all get together and lick stamps?"

"You've got the licking part right," Sarah said with the kind of smile that meant I was now the butt of the joke.

"Um, everybody goes outside after a storm, and— look for the pot of gold at the—" I trailed off. Now everyone was laughing at me.

"You, Jill Soloway, of all people, don't know what a rainbow party is?" Sarah's sister, Becky, asked.

"A rainbow party," Sarah said, digging her hard little piece of bread into the tapenade, "is a party where fourteen-year-olds get together and have lots and lots of oral sex. Each girl wears a different shade of lipstick, and after all the boys get their blow jobs, they've all got rainbows on their penises!"

I felt the buffalo mozzarella coming up in my throat. Fourteen is too young for that many penises. And moreover, why, why why, if these children insist on having oral sex, must it be always be all about the guys? This couldn't be true. But when I got home and googled, I found confirmation.

Or maybe the world had already changed. I've noticed the Porno-ization of America everywhere—at the mall, on *The Bachelorette* and on both of my *Girls Gone Wild* tapes. All of the young modern women of the world look the same. Their hair is blond and flat-ironed, their eyebrows are waxed into inquisitive worms, and their skin is the tawny color of an apple fritter. Either they have implants or wear things in their bras that make them look like they do. With their glossy lips and sullen, black-lined eyes, every last one of them looks fresh from the set of *Meet the Fuckers III*. Lately, everyone I see looks like a hoor.

What happened? When I was a kid in the early seventies, bra-less, gray-haired women appeared to have a lock on things. They had finally unshackled themselves from the shiny girdles, bullet bras, and flippedy hairdos—the Marilynization of America—and they were free. Billie Jean King was whuppin' Bobby Riggs' ass and my mom's friends were marching in the street, calling out for change in deep voices. I believed in the Equal Rights Amendment, and that soon, the black and the white would live together in peace and harmony. I believed War Was Not Healthy for Children and Other Living Things and that by the time I was an adult everyone would be biracial, gender-neutral, and tolerant.

I was too young to know that eras moved in circles, not straight lines, and that once things progressed to a certain point, they would go around the bend and head back, bringing us to where we are today—slaves to our plasmas and SUVs, disciples of our Royal White Family of George and Laura Bush with their Sexy White Offspring, Nick and Jessica Lachey-Simpson.

How did we get back here? It doesn't matter what the good people at *Vogue* and *Jane* have tried to do lately by suggesting that the homeless peasant look is nigh. Real fashion and mall fashion have never been so far-flung. Young girls simply refuse to stop dressing like hoors. Their tube tops and tank tops and jeans are the tightest I've ever seen, way tighter than we wore in the eighties. Ass cracks show, thongs show, as do pierced bellies and hip bones and camel toes, all leading down to a pair of stilettos. Yes, stilettos! Young women of today are wearing stilettos with their denim!

I used to love me a hoor. I've got all manner of second- and third-wave feminist books on my shelves, even including *Whores and Other Feminists*. I was right there when activists switched from picketing sex workers to throwing brunches for Annie Sprinkle. I proudly counted strippers as my friends and touted the idea that the strongest feminist was one who was political *and* who knew how to shake her ass to take men for everything they're worth.

I was even known as a bit of a sex-writer myself, although it had happened without my noticing. I wrote a short story called *Courteney Cox's Asshole* that you may have seen online, but it was dashed out in an hour for the sole purpose of making my friend Becky laugh. Susie Bright, feminist sex writer, just happened to think it was erotica and put it in an erotica collection. I wrote scenes for *Six Feet Under* that were dirty, but they were supposed to be because it's not TV, it's HBO. I just finished a novella that's a sexy coming-of-age diary of a fourteen-year-old girl (in the eighties, no rainbows), but I only wrote it because Susie Bright forced me to.

Indeed, sex as my specialty was a long time in the making, and it wasn't always positive. A few different

TV shows—including the *MTV Movie Awards*—wouldn't hire me because, according to my agent, I had a reputation as "too blue." Sex *had* always been one of my favorite comedic topics, right after explosive diarrhea. I loved putting dirty things in the titles of the plays I directed—*The Miss Vagina Pageant, Not Without My Nipples,* and *Box*—because I knew dirty words were an instant attention-grabber and publicity generator. And, after years of working on sitcom staffs filled with guys, I coolly prided myself on being able to top the dirtiest ass-fucking joke in the comedy writers' room.

Recently, people had even been coming to me, looking for the blue. A few months ago a woman asked me to write a chapter for her collection of essays by Jewish women, on guilt. When I asked her which chapter she wanted me to write, she answered, "Sex."

I suggested I do the Holocaust chapter instead. I told her I was sick of writing about sex and had a brand-new, burning curiosity as to whether I could craft an interesting paragraph without the word "labia" in it. I feared I was a cheap, literary hoor, my work fairly riddled with shiny zirconia piercings. We went back and forth until, finally, I dropped out of the project altogether, probably for the better. I'm sure there are all manner of Jewess begging to go on and on about "My Gigantic Jewish Bush." They should have at it. Me, I'm done. There is nothing left to say about sex. Now, please enjoy my book.

Introduction B
or
He Just Wants
to see Your Panties

Yes, I'm still in my introduction. I promise you there are adorable essays about being me, a mere twenty pages ahead. If the feminist underpinnings to the impending material don't interest you, please move ahead, move ahead to Chapter 1!

Anyway, just one thing before I stop writing about sex forever. I would like to submit to the imaginary court in my head that's judging me constantly that when *I* started writing about sex, it wasn't to be sexy. No sirree. For me, talking about sex in the TV shows and stories I wrote and the plays I produced wasn't only to be shocking or inappropriate. My original intent was something much nobler: inciting feminist revolution.

I have always been a campaigner for words. That's all. More words, written by women, in more books. I was certain that women simply needed to write and contribute to the collection of all things written—as long as it's not a cookbook—and they could change the world. That we would change the world, simply by changing the ratio of stuff made by guys to stuff made by girls. It is an imbalance that drives me, an imbalance I've been aware of since I was seven years old.

On my first day of second grade I nearly had a heart attack when I walked into my classroom. Above me, in a halo around the top of the walls, were pictures of all the presidents. I looked up at the bad cartoony drawings, at the disastrous hairdos and grumpy chins, and knew something was off. Way off. I hoped it was a weird statistical coincidence, as I could tell I was the smartest person in the class, including the teacher. I was certainly smarter than all the boys. So why were there no women up there?

It was clear that something was awry, and that it had been awry for a really long time. Women had been left out of the equation. Since forever. Maybe, I thought, these so-called *men* had taken it upon themselves to make up the rules of the world. Maybe it was *their* dumb idea that rooms should be square and buildings would be tall, and that books were in sentences made of lines. Everything was up for discussion, in my mind. Nothing could be trusted. As the daughter of a feminist, I felt a collective cry urging me on: You, Jill Soloway, set everything right! I decided I'd start by designing round rooms and writing in spirals on purple circular note paper, and not rest until my election as First Woman President of the United States.

My plan to be the boss of everything flourished. It seems no one could tell me anything. Even my father, who wished to tell me how to ride a bike, couldn't. He insists to this day that he wanted to teach me but I *wouldn't let him.* Who cares, I thought, soon I'll be president and just outlaw bike riding. Then somewhere during the fifth grade I got the unfortunate news that a lot of presidents had been in *law.* Shit. That meant passing the bar exam and the bar exam was supposed to be really hard. I guess I couldn't be president after all. My career goals changed, but that didn't stop me from seeing, and more important, *feeling* injustice everywhere.

I was angry, yet queasily ambivalent. I wanted to prove that women could rule the world, yet I refused to stop watching Miss America. I've always loved me a beauty pageant and always will. My sister Faith and I would prepare for hours, making popcorn and cracking open fresh yellow legal pads where we would write down all fifty contestants before the show even started, so we wouldn't get behind during the parade of states. Maybe I was participating in my very own, very early, Media Representation research project. Or maybe my fascination with ermine trumped my political meanderings. Seriously, do you remember ermine? On those red capes they used to wear, trimmed with that fur that looked like slugs crawling up a snow-covered highway?

I had to watch. I couldn't not watch. I enjoyed calling Miss Kansas fat and cheering on Miss Illinois, getting tears in my eyes when she accepted her scepter and crown and moved shakily down the runway. It didn't matter to me that the pinnacle of a woman's life was to be lined up, quantified, and chosen. Things would change soon, and I was going to watch pageants and get in on the action until it did.

Yet watching those pageants aroused at my core an elemental nausea about the very fact of my gender. It gurgled somewhere below my belly and above my crotch, much like acid reflux of the uterus. It made me deeply uncomfortable about a truth I wanted to hide from: that being a woman meant being watched. I wanted to be a watcher, but watching was for the boys.

"Mommy mommy! A boy just paid me a quarter to climb up the telephone pole and down!"

"Silly girl! Don't you know he just wants to see your panties?"

"Mommy mommy! A boy just paid me a quarter to climb up the telephone pole and down!"

"Silly girl! Didn't I tell you? He just wants to see your panties!"

"Mommy mommy! A boy just paid me a quarter to climb up the telephone pole and down!"

"Silly girl! I already fucking told you, he just wants to see your panties!"

"But Mommy! This time I fooled him—This time I didn't wear any!"

Do you remember that joke? Was it passed around your schoolyard too, along with that rhyme about the Chinaman going pee-pee in your coke? This joke had something extra in it that bothered me to my very soul. It went beyond the idea that females were for watching, and introduced the news that men like to watch *without the woman's knowledge.* In fact, poor thing, to this day, I'd bet that pantyless star of the story has no idea the joke was even about her! The foolish pride, the unreturned gaze of the unaware object is what resided at the chewy center of that joke.

Hearing that joke was probably my original scar. What a horrible feeling for someone who knew everything—that the unknowing girl was the true object of desire. The pink, sparkle-sugar coating of her unknowing was the same sugary coating on my most hated enemies—the gleeful, dress-wearing girls: *The Princesses.*

As a child, I heard that other girls were called Princess by their fathers. And I hear shades of it today, particularly from my partner, who's from a red state and another generation. He thinks it's a compliment—in fact, a necessary politeness—to start any encounter with a little girl by proclaiming how beautiful she is.

But here's the worst part. There are some great little girls, kids I really love, the four-year-old down the street, for example, and my three-year-old niece, both of whom are being raised by forward-thinking crunchy liberals. And when my Southern Gentleman boyfriend—who raised two daughters, so isn't open to hearing my opinion on this topic—starts coating these girls in his compliment syrup, something so unnatural happens that it must be instinctual.

"Oh, what a pretty pink dress you have on!" he'll say,

and before I can get to the bathroom to vomit, the little girl lights up brighter than a Christmas tree. A giant grin comes over her face, and the inexplicable spinning starts. It doesn't matter who she is, her hands go out at her sides and her chin tilts up and her eyes scwunch in joy and I feel like a fat fucking feminist grinch who's pissed only because I never got that kind of adoration. I invariably close my mouth, deciding that just because my dad was more interested in anti-Semitism theory books than making little girls feel like princesses doesn't mean I should take that away from the rest of the girl children of the world.

And I surely can't make the case that I never wanted to be an object. I was beset by my very own hunger as the need to be looked at became a colossal pull. By eighth grade I had forgotten what Bella Abzug looked like. I also lost all my smug bossiness. The hands-on-her-hips girl who boldly wore halter tops exposing her big tummy was gone. I traded in my great honking tortoise shell glasses for gas permeable contact lenses and moved across the divide to the ranks of the seen. I got my Ophelia card stamped, relieved to no longer be a seer and do tiring things like think and know.

I forgot about my presidency and everything else I cared about as a young women's libber. My attractiveness was more important to me than anything. This took over and continued, through high school and summers, the loss of my virginity and parties at North Avenue Beach. I was finally good at being female, the right size (four) and the right age (sixteen). My real avocation—writing—was miles behind tanning, dieting, exercising, and shopping, things that helped me with my main hobby, Being Cute.

When I got to college, things changed. It took awhile. The first few years were still all about being adorable. But even while purchasing at least a tube of Bonne Bell Cotton Candy shimmer gloss a week, I found myself fascinated by the Wimmin on campus. Here was a group of chicks who not only didn't shave, but wore tank tops and held long conversations at the Steep and Brew, folding their arms behind their heads and exhaling to make a point. They seemed as happy as anyone I knew—actually, happier—and they weren't being looked *at,* they were looking.

I enrolled in Women's Studies 101. I was lucky enough to have been at University of Wisconsin–Madison during the last reign of one of the greatest, hairiest clans of dyke teachers around. They finally put words to something I'd always felt—that *everything,* everything that had been written and filmed and painted positioned women as the object. And not just in your obvious "women are objects" way. Rather, I began to understand it more the way a sentence is diagrammed—the subject does, the object receives what the subject does. Men were the subjects, of everything.

Now I knew why all those presidents were male. Here was proof that the simple expression of thought had indeed originated with men. It might be about hunting or war or the wind or women, but if we were to exist, it was because a man saw us and put us in his poem. But where were we? Where were our ideas about ourselves and the world? Where and when did we originate, if not in the eyes of men?

I got curious. I got excited. For the first time, I actually went to class instead of buying the notes. I read a bunch and thought a bunch and started to ask questions, the same kinds of questions our books and handouts were asking. There was even one question I felt I was the first person in the world to ask: Why was it so hard for so many women to have an orgasm? And why was it so easy for men?

I explored this in a paper for the class, interviewing all my friends under pseudonyms. My TA, who may or may not have been KD Lang, gave me a C. That's right, a C for the first paper I had written in my entire *life* that had intention and excitement and wasn't copied out of the *The World Book Encyclopedia*.

I went to her crying. She told me I got a C because I didn't include lesbians in my research. Shit. How was I supposed to know lesbians had feelings too? I didn't have any lesbian friends yet, and it was still years before I would find out my own sister was one. KD was not moved by my tears. I didn't know what to do to convince her I was a valid, thinking feminist. I knew she wouldn't take me seriously until the hair on my head was shorter than the hair under my arms.

Introduction C
or
Summer Needs
to Come Already

After the Real Feminists banished me from their midst, I went back to focusing on being cute. But things were starting to look different. I had knowledge. I couldn't just enjoy being looked at without noticing what parts of myself I was giving up. The dichotomies screamed out at me: get dressed up, look away if someone looks at you. Move through the crowded bars in a tight t-shirt, get indignant if a guy brushes past you and gets a feel. Be desirable, never admit desire.

We had always just bought the notion that sex was something boys wanted and girls gave. Gigantic loads of propaganda had been taught to us since forever. High school sex-ed films assured us in fatherly voice-overs that boys think about sex constantly and girls think about it never. Our instructors exhorted us toward success in our main job—to fend boys off, slap hands away and zip up sweaters with a huff. They offered us no evidence that as girls we might want to have sex one day.

We turned to our literature. Okay, we turned to Judy Blume. *Are You There God? It's Me, Margaret* and *Then Again Maybe I Won't* were read in tandem. But Margaret's rite of passage was getting her period, while Joel got to have a wet dream. Finally, Judy wrote about real sex for girls in *Forever,* but Katherine's long-awaited first time came off like a story about someone accidentally farting on her. In college, a few people had that Nancy Friday book they'd stolen from their moms' shelves. But like a poem only as good as it's worst simile, *My Secret Garden* had an unfortunate anecdote involving a peeled banana. And Dr. Ruth, bless her heart, was just too damn short to matter as a sex writer.

What we needed were strong fabulous women we could look up to, women who liked sex and had sex and were still okay. What we needed was *Sex and the City,* but it was still fifteen years in the future. In my worlds—high school in Chicago and college at Wisconsin, amid the sweeping cold plains winds and dairy legacy—admitting you actually wanted to have sex was equivalent to sending out engraved invitations to your very own gang rape.

And the love propaganda drove me nuts. Our main source of information was *General Hospital,* with its Greatest Love Story Ever Told, Luke and Laura. This was a love so fiercely romantic—from the depths of such an infinite truth—that it had to start with a rape. Although Genie Francis' creamery beige skin, emphatic eyebrows, and flat hair foretold today's modern pornified woman, she exemplified what we were all to believe—the only thing women want is Love, Love, Happy Happy Love Love. Men give love to get sex, women give sex to get love.

Finally, in my senior year, I took another class in the Women's Studies Department, in evolutionary biology. This time, I went without any make-up on. I started talking to some of the TAs, pondering more versions of the same old question: Wouldn't the spread of the species be simpler and more straightforward if everyone simply loved having sex all the time? If so, why would our culture evolve in a way to make sex something that it was okay for men to want, but not women? Why were men who had lots of girlfriends envied, while women had to minimize their experience?

One book theorized that male = outside (penis 'n' balls hanging around outside of the body) and female = inside (vagina and distant ovaries, hidden up up and away from the world). Thus, ergo and other words I never heard again after college, male sexuality was simply meant to be outside—seen and known, while female sexuality, at it's most actualized, was hidden.

My new TA, who may have been Joan Armatrading, posited that an exposed, available, come-n-get me vagina projects expectation, simply putting too much *pressure* on that needed-for-evolution erection. Much like a child who can only do the cannonball dive when no one is watching, there's nothing worse for a penis's pride than someone waiting on it.

But my professor had my favorite theory: that everything men do to control the world is based on jealousy. Way back in ye olden days, ancient man saw that not only did women bleed without dying, but also bled in time with the lunar cycle. It didn't matter that men could kill a woolly mammoth; women held an 81-billion-ton trump card—the moon—in their very uteruses. This totally freaked men out, so as epochs passed that I don't have the historical knowledge to fill in, men crafted more ways to make us feel like shit about ourselves. They invented a religion with a male God. To make matters worse they invented another religion where a really cute male God was born to a woman who was so great she got pregnant without even having sex. Now women who resorted to base desire to make babies were heathen and dirty and wrong. The idea of the holy chaste woman was born.

(Please don't try to understand the logic in the above paragraph. I went through epochs very quickly for a reason, combining what I remember from my professor plus stuff I'm making up as I go. Additionally, as long as I'm inside a parenthetical, I've been meaning to explain why this Introduction is still going on: my mom said it was too long. And she was right. Other people told me to cut this part entirely. But I can't, it feels important and I don't know why. If I get my way, Free Press will do a special run with introductions A, B, and C printed on pink transparent plastic instead of paper, maybe even perforated for easy removal.)

Yes, Christianity, and it's worship of a woman for her chastity. To this day, women are forced to teeter on the beams of this ancient triangular equation. A man, the seer of all things, sits at his vantage point at the top of the triangle, looking at two choices. A woman must reside at either of the two remaining available points. She can look away and be the good, beloved Madonna, or return the gaze—see—and be the bad, fucked and forgotten whore. The girl at the top of the telephone pole looked away, ignorant and unknowing, so she was desired. In *Fatal Attraction,* Glenn Close looked back, admitting desire, and had to die.

This push me–pull you festival was ubiquitous. As young women we were always on shaky ground when it came to desire. Even though my friends and I talked about sex all the time, we knew on some level that we had to use indirect means to get it. The main way toward intercourse—outside of a loving, sanctioned partnership—was to follow the script: Smoke too much pot, drink way too much, then find yourself getting talked into it.

If sex did unfold, we knew the worst thing we could do was act too hungry or too experienced. The expected pose was an imitation of a centerfold, wide-eyed, hand over her mouth, afraid and surprised at the erection, wondering, *"What* is that?"

It didn't even matter when time passed and entertainment became a little more liberal—female desire for desire's sake still had to be invisible. In fact, even when *Sex and the City* finally did come on the air, the horny woman profile was relegated to the cartoonish Samantha, while our heroine Carrie made sound judgments, usually only having sex when at least the possibility of love was imminent. Finally, Samantha ended up with breast cancer to punish her years of frolic.

In horror movies, the girl getting fucked in the top bunk of the cabin in the opening scene is always the first to die. In TV cop dramas, prostitutes are routinely bound and burned and slashed. I had a friend who was an actress who swore that all she auditioned for were dark-haired sexy girls who got in car accidents. The message—look for sex and end up raped, dead, or boiling a rabbit.

And if female *desire* was nonexistent or punished in film and on television, the literal portrayal of sexual *satisfaction* was even more elusive. Recently, I was reading a *New York Times* article about what the network censors will and won't allow. It said that on *The OC* this past season, when Seth and Summer were having sex, the network okayed portraying Seth's orgasm but not Summer's. It was so strange to me that a bunch of people in an office could actually hold a meeting and form this idea—yes for his, no for hers. Why? I for one would have loved to have seen Rachel Bilson attempt that acting exercise.

It occurred to me that in some ways we are like Sudan, or wherever those places are in Africa that perform clitoridectomies—female circumcisions. Articles about these mutilations say they are used to control female sexuality by controlling young women. Turns out if you cut off their clits, they don't initiate sex, probably because it's a bit of an ouchy for the first year, and after that, it doesn't feel so good, what with not having a clit and all.

My theory is that keeping women's desire shrouded in secrecy is a metaphorical clitoridectomy. That's right, the genitals of young women are being mutilated every day and it's all Aaron Spelling's fault. I know he didn't create *The OC* but I want to blame him anyway. I have to blame someone. When, oh, when, will we get to feel beautiful, proud, sexual, and free?

I probably should admit my theories are problematic. Just when I've sewn up my metaphorical clitoridectomy argument, I find my arguments are passé. Jenna Jameson and Pamela Anderson are on the bestseller list. Ex-ballerina Toni Bentley's *Surrender,* documenting two years of nothing but anal sex, is called "of note" and "possibly brilliant." Sex-filled paperbacks like Abigail Vona's *Bad Girl,* Catherine's M.'s *Secret Life,* and Melissa P.'s *One Hundred Strokes of the Brush Before Bed* are at the airport bookstore. Porn star, hooker, and stripper have replaced baker, tinker, and tailor as the jobs everyone's writing about. The previously cited Porno-ization of America is not just in the fashions of the high school girls in the food court at the mall, but at the bookstore as well.

So what of my argument? You might wish to pull the previous fifteen pages out, roll them up, and bonk me on the forehead with them. But I don't think I got you all excited about injustice for nothing. Yes, these books are a step in the right direction because they have women's names on the covers. But there's still something that ends up feeling wrong. Toni Bentley just seems like the girl at the top of the telephone pole. I worry about her, that maybe her urge to "bear witness to herself" by describing 217 occurrences of booty-sex was used by a lot of men to convince a lot of women to let them into more places on their bodies. Were her positive responses from men just more boys gathered around the foot of the telephone pole, throwing glowing reviews at her instead of quarters?

And Paris Hilton can hardly be called a sex-positive role model. The quintessential twirling pink princess wore her shy smile, faux-downcast-eyes, hands out at each side, pink nails upturned, as she cried out, "Oopsie! Did you see my special girl place when I accidentally lifted my tutu and you saw that night vision porno tape rolling? Oopsie doopsie daisy!" Naughty Paris carefully put her tiara back on her head, scwunched her eyes up and giggled, then handed in her literary contribution that made no mention of sex at all, just taught us how to pose on the red carpet. Of course, I bought *Confessions of an Heiress* immediately. My love for Paris is like my love for pageants—a Media Representation research project all jumbled up, with purse-puppy envy instead of ermine envy.

I guess I can't have it all. Here I was asking for freedom for more women to write about sex. So who am I to be pissed that other people are having their say first? Maybe my college feminist desire for a lovable whore heroine is finally coming to pass, a meme-like part of the Zeitgeist. Maybe the pink, commercially viable ballerina girls are going to get their say first, making room for *my* kind of sex writing, the super-terrific, really great, keepin' it real kind.

And lest we get too excited about this seeming acceptance of women owning their sexuality, remember that an even bigger bestseller came out, making more money and getting more publicity than all of the previously mentioned Prideful Hoor Collection combined. Called *He's Just Not That Into You,* it manages to reiterate in chapter after chapter that there's nothing a man despises more than a woman who is sexually available to him. Eve Ensler can say we should love our beautiful vaginas and Toni Bentley can go on about how God resides in her anus, but if you're looking for a husband, it still seems best to keep that stuff in your journal and lock it shut.

He's Just Not That Into You reminds us that by putting women's desire up, up and away, hidden from the world, a genetic agenda is winning out. We can't forget that women-owned sexuality contributes to fatherless children. Man-initiated sex and the elusive female orgasm may be an adaptation that rewards men willing to stick around long enough to *convince* the woman to have sex and spend the time it might take to make her come. This naturally selects for men willing to stick around long enough to bring home money and meats and empty the diaper genie, making stable, quality offspring instead of unstable, quantity offspring.

For a man, choosing a woman who desires threatens his paternity. Women know the baby is ours because it came out of us. Men have to just trust that the baby is

theirs. They don't want to find out they've been empty-
ing the diaper genie for nothing all those years. Choosing a woman who enjoys and seeks out sex increases the
chance she may have slept with someone else and that
baby is someone else's.

After figuring this out—that there's an evolutionary
reason (not just a conspiracy) why we find ourselves hating
loose women—it occurred to me that my twenty years of
propagandizing for them might be proof that I'm the An-
tichrist. I asked a good friend. "Seriously," I said. "Do you
think I'm the devil? Tell me. I can handle it."

But my friend just laughed and shook his head and
said that whatever it's called—god or nature or evolu-
tion—it made humans who made condoms and the birth
control pill—which had a lot more to do with sexual
freedom for women than anything else—and it made
Paris Hilton and Jenna Jameson and gave them literary
gifts, and it made the greasy grimy *Girls Gone Wild* girls
and the belly-shirt-wearing high school girls in every
hamlet, and even you, too, Jill.

Perhaps he's right and it made me so I could bring
some balance, change the world. Perhaps it's my mission
to wedge in a little space on the shelves next to the
books by the sugar-coated, shaved-pussy girls. In fact, in
the same way men have historically swung their giant
literary cocks or cupped their massive literary balls, I can
make room for women who wish to openly brandish
their gigantic Jewish literary bushes.

Not that I have a gigantic Jewish bush. I really believe mine's right in the middle, cute as can be and not

at all offensive. So, if you're still on your way to the bookstore to throw this thing in someone's face, you can turn around. There might be some sex in here after all. Also, please wait until you get home to finish reading. I have no idea why you were reading and driving at the same time.

I hope I've made my point. Or maybe a point is something men invented, and, like the writing in circles I imagined in kindergarten, I've written something roundishly holistic that adds up to more of a *whoaaaahhh,* less pointy and more warm, funny, and accepting, like vaginas themselves.

1
Coming Home
(early)

CAMP PINECREST
Every summer, Camp Pinecrest welcomes hundreds of young women from all over the country and the world. Campers ages 6–16 will find a nurturing atmosphere where they can explore, compete, create and discover! Camp Pinecrest provides the tools necessary to grow from a confident young girl into a successful woman.

With over 30 acres of grounds and extensive waterfront property, campers at Pinecrest choose between any number of activities, from swimming in Lake Michigan to learning new crafts in the Recreational Lounge. Pinecrest also offers tennis, basketball, various athletic fields, an obstacle course, and stables, with forty horses.

Camp Pinecrest can accommodate up to 200 girls

(continued on next page)

(continued from previous page)

per session. Campers are assigned a tent cabin, depending on their age. Typically, there are 10–12 campers per cabin and a counselor. Showers and bathrooms are located just a few steps away from the tents–which are equipped with electricity.

Nearby Camp Woodview is our brother camp. Though we share some facilities, activities and experiences at Camp Pinecrest are still strictly female. The two camps do commingle on special occasions during each session. Remember, sessions are filling fast!

When I was twelve my favorite book was about a girl named Marjorie. Marjorie wore pigtails and went to sleepaway camp, with woods and water and tents and friends. I wanted to hang out with Marjorie, or if that wasn't possible, have a life more like hers. Overnight camp sounded like the perfect place to help turn me into a real girl instead of the Formica girl I was becoming in our hi-rise luxury apartment. It was 1977, and we had just moved to the Gold Coast, a neighborhood on the near north side of Chicago.

Ours was a universe of glass, chrome, Berber carpet, and many, many cubes my mom lovingly referred to as Our Parsons Tables. Everything was clean and shiny and in a specific order that never budged. Dinner always featured one of four rotating meats (ground beef, chicken, pork chop, lamb chop, repeat) followed by a Jim Brooks or Burroughs sitcom, then a Pudding Pop. It never changed. Well, to be fair, for a few months in 1982, we tried Tuscan Bars, but returned to Pudding Pops shortly after.

Some deeply longing part of me believed there was something better than the four walls of our air-conditioned splendor, a real place without decorator-chosen taupes and caramels and corners. Even though the capability to google the words "summer camp-Midwest" was two full decades into the future, I was a crafty information gatherer and ordered myself a handbook called *The Camp and School Guide* out of the back of the *New York Times* Magazine section.

After poring over the book for a few days, I found the perfect place: Camp Pinecrest, a couple hours north, in Oconomowoc, Wisconsin. Its brother camp was across the lake and contained boys with whom we would surely share socials and underpants-centered pranking. We asked around the families we knew and found out that Faith's best friend Shelly had been going there for years and loved it. Faith agreed to join me.

"I'm not sure if you're a sleepaway camp person," my mom warned me. But I knew she knew *nothing!* (said haughtily, to self) and had *no* idea about the new me, the me who would soon be whittling things from corncobs and singing, arm in arm, with other real girls. I hovered my hot breath over my mom's shoulder as she filled out the forms. She suggested we start with two weeks and see how it went, but I knew anything less than the full eight would be a disappointment. A week later, the welcome packet arrived, and I sharpened my pencil and began marching around, ticking items off the "Things to Bring" list.

The packet suggested we buy our supplies at a place called the Camp and School Store. It was in downtown Chicago, on the seventh floor of an old-style building on Wabash, all the units darkened by the L trains rushing past outside. The whole entity smelled like dentistry, with elevators that had kindly black men calling out the floors and gates that slid open revealing marble halls and gold-leaf lettering on cloudy white glass doors.

The store was all business: ceiling-high stacks of boxes and forms, forms, forms being checked off everywhere we looked. A pudgy, white-haired Jewish man led us around the store, looking over his half-glasses and pointing at exactly what the list demanded. In reverence to the camp colors, we got Brown and Gold everything—stiff brown shorts, three crusty mustard polo shirts, brown army-issue wool blankets, stiff white sheets, pillow and duffel bag, labels for our names, brown socks, and canteens made of aluminum with brown canvas covers. My mom paid an exorbitant amount of money, and we packed the shopping bags into a cab and went home.

The next week was made up of more planning and meticulous packing. Whenever anyone asked me if I was scared, I'd harrumph and brush them off. After all, my sister would be there and so would Shelly, who I kinda knew, and soon I'd have friends of my own.

When the day came to leave, all of the parents drove their children to a parking lot where everyone bravely hugged good-bye. I hopped on the yellow bus. My sister sat with Shelly and I sat behind them. As they chatted about the eighth-grade girls, I looked around to try to spot the ones going into seventh who would soon be my terrific new bunkmates. The city was leaving us behind and nature, beautiful, real nature, filled the windows as we buzzed up I-94, then off into the north woods of Wisconsin.

We arrived and hopped off the bus. Camp looked exactly how I expected——mossy, meandering paths with leaves everywhere, tall trees and sun-dappled trails to our tent cabins. It was beautiful and crunchy and rustic and it smelled of wet wood. My counselor, a tall, bossy, Naomi-type with big camp thighs and a homemade leather belt, met with my expectations. But sadly, my bunkmates did not. Marjorie was not among them.

They were seven buzzing girls who had known each other since their parents began sending them sleepaway to camp, probably from the age of three. These people were Not Jews. Not at all. But they weren't nature-y either. They were exactly like those old-money blondes with names like Paige and Braeden who went to the private schools in downtown Chicago. They had the hardened, sun-burnt shells of children raised by alcoholic women, left in the yard to play during two-day family parties. Nothing like us Soloway sisters. We were watched like hawks, never out of sight of our mother, never hungry, never bored. I was sure they'd love the way my bubbly personality would provide antidote to their leathered gentile lackadaisy.

Boy, was I wrong. They hated the living shit out of me. Maybe it was my ebullience. But probably, it was my wardrobe. It turned out the Camp and School Store list had just been a SUGGESTED list and not a RE-QUIRED list. As I made my bed with the itchy brown wool blanket, I noticed the rest of the girls had fluffy pink comforters plus sheets pulled from their home linen cabinets, soft as butter, washed weekly since forever.

In addition to their home bedding, each girl also brought mostly regular clothes. Regular clothes. Brown and Gold were only to be worn on Spirit Days, and then only if you were an enormous dork. Certainly not *every* day. And when it *was* Spirit Day, everyone wore lemon yellow cotton scoop-necks and satiny brown jogging shorts with white piping. Like a travel-anxiety night-mare, something had gone wrong in my packing. I had brought almost entirely mustard shirts and cardboard brown army shorts that my mother hadn't even washed first. Just one set of regular clothes. I started crying that night and became known as the Brown-and-Gold Cry-baby to the Seven Shiksas. I had eight whole weeks to get through. But I didn't think I could stand one more second.

Faith, on the other hand, was doing fine, probably dabbling in a burgeoning lesbianism with her best friend, Shelly. Her cabin was chockful of tomboys who took their camping seriously and didn't judge one an-other on things like clothes. Faith loved camp, which should have come as no surprise, as she was incredibly athletic and a great swimmer. I hated things that in-volved rowing and floating, which most things there did. I have no idea why this didn't occur to me when I signed on. Perhaps I should have looked for a camp where girls filled their days with activities like impeccable research, ordering brochures through the mail, and economical packing.

Plus, this place had mosquitoes and bugs and spiders everywhere, including in the toilet and on the toilet seat, and thus, potentially, up my vagina. I was an outcast—the freak in the stiff regulation camp clothes who slept under an army blanket and never peed. In the brutal heat of the Wisconsin summer, I was lonely and boiling and sweaty and sad.

Nothing went right for me. On the second night there, I found myself awake in the middle of the night, outside, lying on the ground. I had no idea how I got there. It turned out I had rolled out of bed in my sleep, and onto the floor, then right out of the space between the tent flap and the bunk floor. I may have slept outside for an hour. I got up, snuck back around to the front, and let myself in while the rest of the girls snored. I slipped back under my hard white sheets, covered in bits of stick, and prayed I would make friends soon with whom I could laugh about such an incident.

But friends were not in the cards for me. The girls not only didn't talk to me, they even appeared to not see me. They lived in a bubble where they held loud private conversations in front of me that left no way in. They never specifically bullied me, they just behaved as if I wasn't there. In fact, I bet if you found any of these Paiges or Braedens today, they wouldn't even remember me.

My loneliness was overwhelming and my crying myself to sleep wasn't attracting the attention it was supposed to. Even though my sister was at the same camp, our paths didn't cross. I was campaigning to get them to let me sign up for an all-indoor day, a triple class in Lanyards followed by two sessions of Advanced God's Eye. Faith was out getting Best New Water-skier medals and captaining a Sunfish solo.

Between activities, Faith and I could find very little time to talk. I finally arranged a meeting with her at the Canteen (not the silver ones with the brown covers but the one where you could buy a candy bar and stamps, like prison). I had hoped Faith would hug me and introduce me to some eighth graders who might wish to take me under their eighth-grade wings. But as soon as she saw my tears she gave me an excuse about having to get to the stables to muck out her new horse, Lucky, and made a mad dash. It turned out Faith was thrilled to finally have some friends who didn't know about her association with, apparently, the biggest crybaby in the world, me. Away from home and our mom's sweet inclusiveness rules, she didn't have to pretend like she cared.

The last straw came on day four, when my counselor—who was supposed to protect me from my meangirl bunkmates—pointed out to them something they hadn't noticed. She made fun of the way I was eating. I guess I pushed my food onto my fork with my fingers instead of my knife. I still do this today, having picked up this shtetl-fabulous habit from my parents, who for some reason, have no idea how to eat. At my table, Paige, Braeden, and crew knew how to use *both* pieces of silverware. They thought they were so big. The waterworks started again. I looked around to find Faith, but she had her back to me. I feigned a stomach flu and went back to the cabin to lie down.

The next morning I went to the camp director, Miss Wurher, who the rest of the year played the banker Miss Hathaway on *The Beverly Hillbillies.* I told her to call my parents—that I was going home. She brought me to the screened-in camp office and showed me the phone, certain my mom would comfort me by telling me how strong I was and that I would get through it. She obviously had never met my mom, a woman whose parenting style could be boiled down to one sentence, repeated lovingly to me and Faith on the hour throughout our childhood: *"Whatever your little hearts desire."* My mom told me she was on her way. I hung up the phone and smiled smugly at Miss Wurher.

A few hours later my parents were there with a silver Volvo and an empty trunk. Miss Wurher scowled and suggested the three of us go for a walk. My dad got out a can of Off, sprayed us all down, and we followed her into the woods. She led us to a stump and a log in an area that may have been called The Sharing Glen.

"I really must tell you," Miss Wurher said liplessly, "that if Jill goes home from camp early, it will be a mistake she will regret for the REST OF HER LIFE."

The rest of my life. Wow. That was heavy. Could this bitch in the brown poly pants be right? She didn't even know me. And she obviously hated Jews. I did my best to dismiss her. I stared at the way the sun made patterns on my shoes. I looked at my dad's sandals, and his black socks against his hairy white legs. I contemplated the internal life of a nearby potato bug.

My parents stood up. "We appreciate your opinion, but we disagree," my mom smiled, and we all headed for the car. My dad had missed most of the conversation, because, as usual, he was listening to a Cubs game, with a skin-colored knob in his ear and beige cord down his shirt and into his pants pocket. In retrospect, he was actually a very forward-thinking early iPod advocate, the first person I knew to spend time in between his ears in public.

In fact, throughout my entire childhood, my dad was always listening to a Cubs game. Most of the time he did it covertly, only causing trouble during one of my sister's high school orchestra recitals when, during a sotto movement, he screamed out, "Run You Fat Bastard!"

Trying to hide my smile from Miss Wurher, I followed my parents back toward the main office and to the car. Once the doors were closed and we were on our way, I cried and cried, this time pink and purple tears of joy, not brown and gold tears of shame. When we got to the air-conditioned splendor of our downtown Chicago apartment, I knew I would never go anywhere again, and that the ABC lineup—*All My Children, One Life to Live,* and *General Hospital*—plus a Lean Cuisine for lunch and another for dinner, were the perfect summer program for me.

I had our apartment and my mother to myself for the rest of the summer. When Faith finally came home, she was tan, had long, thin tennis muscles in her arms, and a woven headband in her hair. I was bloated from the

Stouffers salt content, happy, and pale. I didn't care. I knew Miss Wurher was wrong and that it wasn't a mistake at all. I was sure there'd be other travels and new adventures, places that were mine, where I would know how to stay, instead of run.

COSTA RICA

With beaches stretching across most of the country and spring-like temperatures all year round, Costa Rica offers the perfect vacation environment. Though the tumultuous climate of its neighbors has ruined much of the tourism industry in Latin America, people from all parts of the world continue to flock to Costa Rica. It has enjoyed a reputation of being beautiful and safe, making it one of the most popular destinations for women traveling alone.

If you're looking for adventure, there are active volcanoes, waves suitable for world class surfing, and lush jungles to explore. Many endangered species of birds and animals find solace on Costa Rican soil, thanks to the country's progressive policies on conservation.

But Costa Rica is also a place to sit back, relax, and unwind in the warm coastal breezes and bright sunshine—but be careful, time tends to disappear in paradise!

Some time after college I decided it was time for me to finally write my first book. I decided I'd better start getting some Real Experiences under my belt, on my way to becoming the next Kerouac, or better yet, the First Female Kerouac. (By the way, if any boys reading this aspire to be the First Male Soloway, I say, go for it.)

My boyfriend at the time was a British guy named Nigel whose nickname for me was Pudge. Nigel was not a nice fellow. Whenever anyone asked me to describe him, the only answer I could think of was, "Exactly like the Max Von Sydow character in *Hannah and Her Sisters* but meaner and younger." After our first date, any normal woman would have said, "You never speak, and when you do, it's only to insult me, my beloved television, and the United States. Thank you, but I'd rather not get together again." Instead, I stayed with him for four years. When I couldn't stand him any longer, rather than break up with him, I arranged this trip to another land. My plan was to come back stronger, like a real person who went places and did things, like a real writer. Like someone with the backbone to say something as simple as, "This isn't working out."

When I chose to escape to Costa Rica, it was because of books again. The first was a guidebook. Jesus, I love me a guidebook. Such nicely organized information. Regions are divvied into reasonable, doable chunks. They promise adorable cafés, taunt you with the word "pensione," and have sections called "For Women Traveling Alone," as if that's a reasonable thing to do.

The other half of the blame goes to a book by Mary Morris, called *Nothing to Declare,* found in the cheapie bin at Kroch's and Brentano's. Just as I wanted to be more like Marjorie the camp girl, I'd graduated to envying the life Mary described in her books. Mary was partial to South America and made repeated references to huts and gentle foreign lovers and plump women who taught her how to hang laundry on twine handspun from banana leaves. Latin America sounded scary, but everyone said Costa Rica was like a cute, doll version of Latin America. In fact, in Costa Rica, the national word is "Tico," and you know what? Tico means friend!

I was a freelance production assistant so I had some money saved and no work for a few weeks. I made my move very quickly. I ordered a last-minute cheap plane ticket over the phone and announced to everyone that I would be leaving that Friday. I truly have no idea why no one stopped me. My mom didn't wave my camp experience in front of me, although Nigel looked up from his dark beer long enough to say, "You'll never make it, Pudge." My dad was still listening to the same Cubs game. So I made a list and shopped, bought blank books to write in, and nylon pocket things for my documents. I packed everything perfectly in my brand-new backpack and went, by myself, at the age of twenty-three, to Costa Rica.

When I arrived it was late at night. I caught a cab to one of the places *Let's Go Costa Rica* said was clean and lovely and Young Travelers Congregated. Time to begin my adventures. I walked in the door of the hostel. It was hideous, and fluorescently lit with waxy linoleum tile floors, slick with the stench of cheap disinfectant. It was like checking into a foreign hospital for no good reason. There were no travelers sitting in a klatch playing guitar and inviting me to join them, so I went to my room and went to sleep.

I awoke the next morning jet-lagged and confused. What was I supposed to do now? I grabbed my duffel bag and went through the lobby. I walked into town and sat in a café, and cracked open my fresh travel journal. Yes, I was a subject now, not an object! I was Kerouac! Costa Rican men were standing at a counter drinking shots of espresso, and I hadn't seen that before, so I wrote it down. And waited. For another thought. Anything to write about. I hadn't even gotten through the first page and I was done. I closed the book and buried it deep within my bag so I wouldn't have to see it again. It would be the first of many beautiful, leather-bound journals, empty save page one.

I went outside and saw a lot of multi-colored buses and sixties-style architecture and inhaled thick black bus fumes. I wondered where the tortoises and monkeys and thatched-roof huts were. I got on a bus to go somewhere I'd read about.

But it soon became obvious Costa Rica was unwilling to share with me her waterfalls and palm fronds. My whole trip is a memory of running, getting to a town, checking in somewhere, not knowing what to do, checking out, reading the guidebook, finding a hut, finding it full of cockroaches and Australians, running again. I finally made a friend but decided I couldn't stand her mere hours later. I finally found a tour that would take me to the jungle but changed my mind because one last warning sign foretold rigorous physical demands. I knew what rigorous meant.

Happily, I also knew what resort meant. I opened my

guidebook and flipped to the section. I didn't have much money left, but I had my parents' credit card and I knew how to use it. When we were kids, every last week of August, our family had gone to an expensive resort in Mexico or Jamaica. This was something I could do.

I took a taxi to a giant concrete ugly sixties pyramid-shaped hotel. The lobby had more linoleum, this time disguised as marble. I didn't care. I checked into my room and breathed a sigh of relief. Ahhhh. No more stinky buses or hairy travelers or orange drinks in dirty bottles. This place had room service, and a pool. I changed into my bathing suit and went downstairs, jumping in within seconds. Again with the ahhhhh. I paddled around a little, got out, ordered a banana daiquiri and lay flat on a chaise. Yes.

No. Within a half hour I was drunk and burnt bright red, skin afire and bubbly. I guess I missed the part in the guidebook about Costa Rica being near the equator and all. I stumbled back to my room, applied aloe vera everywhere, then made a sticky hovel for myself under the starchy sheets, alternately cold and feverish. It felt like the worst flu I ever had. I cried. The next day my skin peeled off in sheets like dried Elmer's glue and I was ready to run again. But I couldn't go home. I had done Camp Pinecrest for four days; I needed to at least get past that.

I got on a bus to anywhere. Next to me was a young couple. The girl placed her hand on the boy's thigh, palm up, and I watched as it casually bounced with the rhythms of the bus on the bumpy road, telling the world she belonged to someone. The sight grabbed my heart, and I got off the bus and called Max von Sydow to tell him I missed him more than life itself and to please come and meet me in Torteluga. He told me to grow up and tough it out. I imagined him in Chicago wearing Miss Wurher's soft-perm hairdo and brown polyester pants.

After exchanging numerous "I Love You More's" with the man I despised, I hung up. I didn't know what to do or where to go. I paged through my guidebook. I came across a listing about an American who helped travelers find accommodations with local families. Hmmm. This sounded good. When I dialed the phone, little did he know the only acceptable thing he could have done was drive straight to me with a silver Volvo and an empty trunk. Instead he gave me the name and address of a lovely family who rented out rooms to travelers, and called ahead so they'd expect me.

I took a taxi a few towns away, clutching the address, determined this would be the Native Experience for which I'd come this far. We twisted and turned down streets with addresses ordered something like 1, 88, 3, 88, 765, 14, 88, and 14. Turned out they used the Random and Repeated system to number homes in Costa Rica. The driver finally found the house and dropped me off.

The host family was lovely enough but sadly, also had a linoleum floor and used too much cleanser. Nothing smelled like incense or wood or the way I wanted my Latin American experience to smell, just bug spray and cheap disinfectant. The family showed me to a room with a frayed bedspread. Ol' Brown-and-Gold Crybaby lay down and had at it again, snuffling her tears into the nubs of the chenille.

That night, we ate an awkward dinner of Beans and Rice with Delightful Gristle. I thanked my new family effusively and told them in my college Spanish how happy I was that I finally found a place in Costa Rica that felt like home, a place where I could just relax and use it as a base and really start to explore the country. Then I went back to my room and fell asleep at six-thirty.

I awoke at three in the morning, alert as a cat. Time to run. My host family snoozed, unaware their new guest was goin' on the lam. I wrote them a note in halting Spanish. It said *"Tico, no esta usted, es mi,"* which I'd hoped meant "Friend, it's not you, it's me," but I now realize may have meant, "Friend, you're not you, you're me." Then I waited and watched out the window.

Soon the sun rose. In the distance, I saw a taxi go by. Then another. Then another. This was good. Taxis came here. I grabbed my bag and snuck out the front door, running like a kid who'd just left a pile of burning doo-doo on their doorstep. I hailed the taxi and went to a pay phone. This time I was smart. I called my mom instead of Max von Sydow, and she told me that if my little heart desired to come home early, my little heart should come home early. I went to the airport and feigned an emergency stomach flu to a reservations agent and she arranged for me to get on the next plane.

I had about an hour to wait. I passed a room with a sign that said CHAPEL and went in, hoping to squeeze in my transcendent travel experience. I pushed open the heavy door to find . . . more fluorescent light and linoleum. Someone should really put that in the guidebook: Costa Rica! Come for the Fluorescent Light and Linoleum!

I sat in a pew and looked up at the mommy who was going to have to be good enough until I could get home to my nice soft Jewish one. I think she was the Virgin Mother Mary or some such. I get confused and don't know why everyone is named Mary in Catholicism. Who's Magdalene? Which one was the prostitute? Which one was Jesus' mom? I don't know. If some of these chicks were named Kimberly or Donna it would help.

An hour later I was on the plane, and five hours after that I was home, sweet home. It was years after camp and so my mom's browns and tans had been traded in for art deco pinks and grays, but the couch felt just as good. I promised myself and the world, I would never go anywhere again.

I spent the next few days watching *All My Children* and eating Lean Cuisines, and soaking up the air conditioning and velour pillows. God, was I happy. I may have been ruined for life, but at that moment, for all I cared, Miss Wurher could eat my snatch while Max von Sydow and the Costa Rican host family watched.

To close, if *this* book helps one person not travel, it will have been worth it. That's right, unlike Mary Morris or *Let's Go*, Jill's book says: Let's Don't Go, Okay? Seriously, don't. Go anywhere. Television is plenty interesting. Also, women shouldn't travel alone. No one should, not even men. It's really lonely. If you have to travel, travel with someone. Also, sleepaway camp sucks, especially Camp Pinecrest, where the woman who runs it, Miss Wurher, is a big fat stupid Jew-hating bitch.

2

Tiny Ladies in Shiny Pants

I'm getting nervous.

My heart is beating, way too fast.

I can see her, at the end of my street, and she's coming this way. Oh god, here she comes, is it true? Here she comes.

Her name is Rebecca and she lives just down from me in the hilly roads of Silver Lake. She's my friend Rob's girlfriend, and she's in this band called Becky, so, it's weird—it's my natural instinct to call her Becky instead of Rebecca, right? But it turns out she doesn't like being called Becky. So I asked her, you know, that being the case and all, if she really thought that calling her *band* Becky was a good idea, or if, at least, she should consider breaking the moratorium on people calling *her* Becky.

She smiled, then laughed, then said that could be a good idea.

I smiled.

We smiled, and it was awkward. And then it was over. I went home and showered off gallons of sweat. That was the last time I saw her, about a month or so ago. And here she comes again walking her dog and I will have to think of something to say, try to figure out some way to act normal in her presence.

Maybe you're wondering why I'm behaving this way. I'm not sure if the name Rebecca sounds familiar to you, but it should, because THIS IS THE REBECCA FROM FUCKING *REAL WORLD SEATTLE*!!!!!!!!!!!!!!!!!!! and I am not lying! Do you remember Rebecca? She had white blond hair and greenish eyes, she went into the music studio and put on some cans so she could lay down some tracks???!!!! With Sir Mix-A-Lot? Anyone? Rebecca from Seattle *Real World*??!!

I am a starfucker. I am a fuckin' star fucking starfucker. There is nothing I love more than a star, except a reality star, which proves nothing except that I'm disturbed in a very special way. You would think I would rather have lunch with George Clooney than Amaya from *The Real World Hawaii* but you would be wrong.

Celebrity has always been more important to me than anything. My whole career started because my sister and I did a play about the *The Brady Bunch,* which was just so I could meet Eve Plumb. When I eventually got my conversation with Eve Plumb, it was mostly just sad, like talking to someone with those eyes that suggest they were raised in a war-torn region.

Even before we created the *Brady Bunch* play, I'd put

a lot of thought into fame. I wanted to make a documentary about how it felt to be a Brady. I imagined that it was really hard to be Eve Plumb, or any celebrity for that matter. The most tragic-seeming part to me was what it must have felt like to not only lose anonymity, which was obvious, but, more important, to lose moments of possibility, often the very magic of life. At that time, I knew that if I—anonymous Jill—walked into a bar and someone turned and looked at me, and our eyes met, any number of thoughts could run through my mind: Who is this person? What are they staring at? Is this my soul mate? A special teacher of a special life lesson? A freak? A new friend?

For a celebrity, all of that's gone. I wanted to interview Eve Plumb and ask her what it felt like to never again have the chance to be "Who is that?" and forever be "That's Jan!" Even worse, "That's Jan!" could only be followed by disillusionment, because she wasn't Jan, she was Eve. Eve had not spent the same amount of time with the fan as the fan had spent with Jan. She'd never have the requisite amount of interest in the fan, and would always be only a disappointment. That's what I wanted to ask her, "Say, Eve, how does it feel to be a great big disappointment to everyone you meet?" Luckily I never made that documentary.

I had a theory that as shitty as life might be for celebrities, they served a very important purpose. They were our modern day replacements for Greek gods, particularly in their multiplicity, which was lacking in the Judeo-Christian singular God. Instead of Athena and

Apollo, we had Farrah and Lee Majors. Rather than pray to Eros for love, we'd read a story in *People* about Brad Pitt. I could understand why adults would desire this ascension, and could see how badly stage parents would want it for their children, even against better judgment.

But now that I've spent time around famous people, stardom appears to be less a need to ascend, than an urge to regress, to infancy. Stars, in all actuality, are great big babies. Forget walking into a bar alone. You're never, ever alone when you're famous. You've always got your nanny with you, in the form of a publicist or a posse. Stars get to reclaim the special feeling that we haven't had since we lay on our back in a pram, people approaching to see the adorable baby, cooing, "Hello! Well hello there! I see you! Yes I do I do I do I do, I see you yes I do! Oh you're such a good baby and a good smiler with one toof! Look at your one toof! Yes I see your one toof!"

The constant head-turning that stars attract is the closest thing to returning to that delectable über-importance. The giant bodyguard is like an ever-present, ever-vigilant good version of Daddy. The paparazzi are Grandma and Grandpa, demanding to snap more, more, more pictures of baby.

If you've ever seen an actor in the hair and makeup trailer you'd know it's like a great big changing table. Hands come at the big babies with wet-wipes. They get their hair combed and spritzed and sprayed, then patted flat with a firm hand, neck-chilling amounts of attention given to even one errant strand. People constantly want to know if they're comfortable, bringing cashmere blankets and three new pairs of Uggs to choose from. On one show I worked on, when one of the lead actresses sat in the hair chair, she clutched a hot water bottle with a fur cover, like a real live, living, breathing hot teddy bear. I want to clutch a hot water bottle all day. I want a hot water bottle placed on all parts of me, all day.

Of all the actors I worked with, this one fascinated me the most. I would watch her from afar, waiting on the set. She seemed so content, like the biggest happiest baby in the world. I loved the way she sat with her feet propped up, waiting for someone to tell her what to do next, leaned back in a director's chair with her name on it like it was ordered out of a Lillian Vernon catalog Especially for Her. Clutching her furry hot water friend who emanated a moist heat, and covered by her blankey, she welcomed the few she liked with overbearing, entitled intimacy, then ignored the rest with toddler-style imperious, haughty dismissal. And who could blame her? Adults are all manners, no boundaries; children and celebrities are all boundaries, no manners, which sounds much less exhausting.

People bring stars great cups of sweet creamy things from Starbucks to drink from a straw, then stand by to take the cup back if they don't feel like holding it. Stars get plates of bacon, just bacon—if that's what they wish for, the way a baby refuses to eat anything but hot dogs for a week. If the crew is eating from the lunch truck and big baby prefers sushi, big baby gets sushi.

Whether it's about an ascendance to the heavens or a

regression to the anal stage, losing myself in fame has always been an endless source of interest for me. *People* and *US* is the practice of my religion, like meditating on rosary beads. Like driving, it holds onto just enough of my brain so I can relax, leaving the rest of me to breathe evenly, the way I'm supposed to.

It was clear from the moment I was old enough to focus that there was one Most Important Ever, glassy-square-eyed Alpha Male member of our family—the television. My sister and I stared at him for six hours a day after school, our pupils buzzing, brains overstimulated. My mother kept an eye on him as she weighed her Puffed Rice into a scale each morning. And I knew that if I was inside that box (and wearing a Cubs uniform), there was a chance my father might look at me when he got home from work.

My mom is the original starfucker. She has always believed everything she read, a devoted out-loud repeater of boldfaced tidbits of news in the *Chicago Sun-Times* about local celebs like Phil Donahue. In fact, she even uses the words "local celeb" conversationally.

She was a PR person by occupation as well as obsession. Her days were spent angling for press placements for her clients. Nothing happened unless it was written about. Our lives paled in comparison to the lives of those who demanded coverage. As soon as I was old enough to move about the city on my own, I gravitated toward places where I could meet stars.

I blame my young stalking habits on my eighth grade best friend. Our family had just moved to a new neighborhood, called the Gold Coast, and I didn't know anyone at my new school yet. Fresh from the soul trampling I'd received at summer camp, I was ready to be friends with the first person who'd have me. Her name was Luisa.

Regular life bored Luisa. She blew off school all the time, because she had nothing to lose. She lived in a cramped apartment with her chain-smoking mother and stories about her French chef father. At only thirteen, she was quickly developing a punk-rock misanthrope pose that drew me in. I was getting tired of my array of kelly green cable-knit sweaters, and in my never-ending search for identity, I was more than happy to cut school with her the day the Cars came to town.

It was 1978. Luisa was in love with Cars guitarist Elliot Easton, and felt certain that he would love her too as soon as they met, if only she had the right clothes. Luckily, Fiorucci had just opened up at Water Tower Place, our local mall. In the dressing room, I hunched near the floor as she changed into the pants that would become the center of her wardrobe and the marker of a moment in fashion that would begin anew—purple satin supertight peg-legs. If you're freaking out right now about how to integrate what I just told you about the cable knits, please understand that even though we were preps, we wore our sweaters with supertight peg-leg Gloria Vanderbilts *and* leg warmers, so it wasn't a HUGE stretch to try on such a pant. The cut was familiar; it was the sheen that was new.

As Luisa turned this way and that, her miniature hip bones jutting out from the shiny violet waistband, she explained to me exactly how we would get to meet the Cars.

"We get their last album, then look for the name of their tour manager. Then we call the big hotels—Drake, Whitehall, Ritz. If you ask for Elliot Easton, they'll know what you want, but if you ask for Rod Howell—he was the tour manager last year—they'll connect you right away."

We paid for Luisa's new clothes, then went back to her smoke-sodden apartment. First, Luisa made me pick my Cars boyfriend off the album cover to assure her I wouldn't try to steal Elliot Easton. All five of them had mullets, which actually looked hot back then. Ric Ocasek's imposing nostrils intimidated me, so I chose Ben Orr. Luisa picked up the phone. We tried the Whitehall first, and the operator put us right through to Rod Howell's room. Luisa hung up quickly.

"Oh my god," she said. "I found them."

In her tiny vomit-pink and gold-speckled bathroom, Luisa lit a match to melt the end of her eyeliner. The smoke from the sulfur danced as she shook it out, then blew on the tip and drew the liquefied brown into cat-eye extensions of her little girl eyes.

"Don't act like a dork, okay?" she said. I promised I wouldn't embarrass her. She changed into her new clothes, pinned on a few buttons—PIL and one with red script on black saying *Police* (who were still a punk band)—and we headed out. I didn't have the street cred to wear punk clothes yet, so my Calvins, Candies, and a striped angora sweater had to do.

We walked the three blocks to the tony Whitehall hotel. My apartment, her apartment, our school—everything was in superclose proximity. When we moved here from the rambling south side with its train tracks and rail yards, it was like landing in a wee, lovely version of Manhattan—tall buildings, taxis, hustling and bustling stores, but on a small scale. We had our boundaries—never go south of Randolph, north of Armitage or west of Wells, with the east being the lake—so our entire sophisticated world lived within a one-and-a-half-mile radius.

When we got to the Whitehall there were some greasy, autograph-seeking weirdos waiting outside, clutching 8 x 10s and markers. We certainly weren't with them. We were different. We sat on the couch in the lobby, chatting like out-of-town guests. The elevator doors opened, and out they came. We resisted the impulse to jump up and tackle them. They passed right by us—goose-like Ric Ocasek, Luisa's one true love Elliot Easton, and my one true love Benjamin Orr, whom I couldn't pick out of a lineup tomorrow if you threatened murder, or something even worse, like cancelling my *In Touch* subscription. We followed them through the foyer and onto the street.

Jesus. Now, there were groupies outside—little girls, mere children. Nothing like us. The little girls screeched as Ric, Elliot, and Ben brushed past. We followed close behind, rolling our eyes at the inconvenience of the screaming fans, amid a faux conversation about which was the fastest way to the Art Institute—a taxi or the L

train. Luisa remarked that perhaps walking to the Art
Institute on a day such as this would be lovely, quite
lovely, and I agreed.

In a moment we were inches behind them, and Luisa
loudly remarked that the Buzzcocks show at the Park
West was killer. We stayed close on their heels, Candies
clacking, satisfied that our first encounter allowed them
to see us as equals and left them wanting more, so much
more. We were sure they were blind to our mouthfuls of
braces and our glasses with oversized frames that can
only be described as pink tapioca tortoise shell.

Our husbands took a right on Michigan Avenue,
also known as the Magnificent Mile. And this was indeed magnificent, for they were going to Water Tower
Place, our mall! Once in, they made a beeline straight
for Fiorucci—*our store!* We had so much in common
with them already! At Fiorucci, we hovered nearby. A
salesgirl, who obviously thought she was a real friend
to the Cars instead of a fan like us, pointed to us and
laughed. This was humiliating. We were Fiorucci shop-
pers, not stalkers! To prove our point, we walked out
without even turning around. Ha. We sure showed the
Cars.

As eighth grade continued we got better at our
game, meeting Cheap Trick, The Knack, Rod Stewart,
and, climactically, Van Halen. For Van Halen, we'd
snuck into the upstairs hallway of the Ritz-Carlton by
following a tourist into the elevator. We asked him if he
had seen a band. "I think I saw some people from Van
Heflin on the tenth floor."

Moments later we found David Lee Roth coming out of his room. He assumed we wanted autographs, and so autographs it was. It seemed a little late to convince him that he should consider marrying one of us. He had a ballpoint pen and grabbed my arm, writing his name on it.

"David . . . Lee . . . Roth . . . there," he said, handing my arm back to me roughly. "When you get home today and your mom asks you what that means, tell her it means . . . (dramatic pause) ROCK AND ROLL!!!!!"

Excuse me? MOM? What in the world made him think we had moms? We were tiny ladies! Yes, in shiny pants! Well, one of us anyway. I was still too chicken to make a fashion statement outside of my Gloria Vander-bilts. But Luisa was shiny enough for the both of us. We scowled at stupid David Lee Roth's insult and decided that, as long as we had nothing better to do, we may as well go back to school so Mrs. Smeriglio wouldn't make us take the spelling test over on Monday. We figured we could blend in when the after-lunch bell rang and all the kids were coming back from Bagel Nosh.

In the following years Luisa got angrier and started wearing more black eyeliner and actually going to punk shows. My parents didn't let me do that, but I kept up my stalking ways with my new high school friends. My friend Angela and I moved on to actors, searching out Brooke Shields, Christopher Atkins, and Matt Dillon. Why Brooke Shields, you might ask. Clearly, she would never be your husband. But it wasn't autographs we craved. We just knew that a day where you had seen

Brooke Shields up close was better than a day you hadn't.

One afternoon, we were hanging in the lobby of the Hyatt so Angela could meet her boyfriend Sean Penn who was in town filming *Taps*. When it looked like we'd missed him, we adjourned to the game room for some Ms. Pac-Man to cheer us up.

A shy, pretty boy was in there playing Galaga. Angela asked him if he had seen Sean Penn, and he told us that he hadn't but he hoped to meet him soon—it was his very first ever acting job and he was going to have one line in *Taps*. "Cool," Angela said. "Well, give me your name and number, just in case you're famous one day."

The boy got out a scrap of paper and wrote down his name and home phone number. He smiled big white teeth at us, then left. Angela remarked that he was a loser.

"What was his name?" I asked. She got out the paper and read it. "Tom Cruise."

"Huh," I said. "Maybe if he wasn't so short we'd call him." And yes, one day, a few years later, I asked Angela if she still had that paper, but she couldn't find it. Oh well.

As I got older, I kept trying to meet stars. I had read in the *Sun-Times* that Billy Dee Williams was in town to film a movie. I had always thought he was sexy, so I called the old stalwart, the Whitehall, just to find out if he was there. He was. I put on the fake husky voice of a lady, to see if he would talk to me. He invited me to come right on over. I said I'd probably better not because I was sixteen. He considered this for a moment and then agreed it would be better if we just talked on the phone. Right before he hung up, he checked again, "Are you sure you're just sixteen?"

Every time famous people came to Chicago, I managed to find them. After Angela switched to horses, I switched to Neille. My relationship with her started like she was the star and I was the stalker. She was the most beautiful girl in our school—a cheerleader *and* a teen model, the lost sister of Jessica and Nicole Simpson. When we met on the first day of my freshman year, her opening line to me was, "What are you, some kind of a prep?" I didn't care that she was insulting me, I just wanted to be in her aura.

When I was with Neille, famous people wanted to be in our aura. (And just so you hear it right in your head while you're reading, Neille is not Nelly. It's pronounced like a boy's name—Neal. Except when guys didn't get it, she would say, "Neille. Like on your knees. Kneel!" She was that cool.) Bill Cosby came over to our table at a restaurant and asked if he could join us. After lunch, he offered us a ride home. Craig T. Nelson offered to buy us drinks at a restaurant in the middle of the morning. Reggie Theus, who was, at the time, a Chicago Bull, invited us to join him at some pro-basketball parties. Once I got to college, even without Neille at my side, I knew who the celebrities were. I made sure to "date" the football players and star basketball player, even though I'm sure they never knew my last name and possibly may not have known my first.

And when I got out of college and into advertising, it was in hopes of meeting famous people. When we shot commercials on location and looky-loos would come up to watch, we'd call the camera the Asshole Magnet. But the joke was on us. They wanted to check it out for five minutes, but *we* were the assholes who couldn't live without it, had to be right next to it every single day. After considering making that documentary about searching for Eve Plumb's humanity, I fell into directing and producing *The Real Live Brady Bunch,* a play that was a TV show. And now, finally, I write on a real TV show.

There are all kinds of renowned, smart playwrights working with me on *Six Feet Under.* When we walk to the cafeteria together, people think we are all the same—people who say they love the *written word* with rolled r's. And maybe on my good days I approach that. But most of the time, I know that being a TV writer allows me to do something I've always longed to do—stick my hand up the crotch of that giant TV and make those dolls talk. It's my deep dark secret—that the actors are my big Barbies and it's all just a dolls game. I may never lose the twenty pounds I would need to lose to be on TV. But at least for now, I'm in the TV.

And luckily, my thirst for star proximity has been somewhat eased as I've grown up a little. These days I generally won't leave my house simply to meet a star at a party. My job at *Six Feet* allowed me to stalk Ellen De-Generes by writing her into an episode. Plus I have to act cool around stars, what with the fact that I have to talk to them about the script sometimes, so I pretty much keep that part of myself to myself. Fortunately, by the time this book comes out we'll be wrapped and I won't run into Lauren Ambrose, Peter Krause, Rachel Griffiths, Jeremy Sisto, or Michael C. Hall. God forbid they should read this and know that every time I ever spoke to them I was secretly schvitzing.

It's weird. I'm not like this with most people. I can talk my little brain off with fancy famous directors about ideas. I could meet writers I love; I could meet Jonathan Ames, the man who I would want to take me to the prom if there were a high school called Humorous Essayists North, and not be nervous, just excited to share my personality with him, my personality that I am certain he would love. I could meet anyone recognized for any *intellectual* pursuit, and I would not be intimidated. But I get nutty and nervous, just nutty-ass nervous, around stars.

Surely most have heard the maxim that we fear what we secretly love. Perhaps this is why I fear the Celebrity. Maybe, behind everything I do, every word I write, even those words you just read, and, now, slow down . . . this word—*WORD!* there's the wish to be known by millions. Why else would I obsessively Google myself? Remember when, if you had a few minutes to spare, you might engage in secret diddling? No more. Now, when no one's around, I shamefully masturgoogle. I'll type my name in, with and without quotes, even misspelling it to see if anyone else has. Even if people write mean stuff, I like it. It's like staying in the bathroom all day long in high school reading the walls to see if anyone has written "Jill Soloway is a bitch."

Google gives me a hard number (today it's 1,560)—a real measurement of my reach. Sometimes I e-mail a quick thank-you-for-increasing-my-googlability to a blogger, hoping they'll mention the thank you, adding another page to my number. This obsession completely confounds me. The circularity of my arguments that I'd hoped to pass off as holistic and feminine is even more apparent here. You may have noticed I'll do that—wave a flag, then frantically run across the street, yelling, "Hey! I'm over here now!"

Remember, for example, in Introduction A, when I postulated an entire theory that the pain of being a woman is really the pain of being Seen before getting a chance to See? Now that I'm writing a book, albeit one articulating how everything I do is a cry for recognition, I endanger the non-object status for which I've worked so hard. I even have a publicist in this literary exercise in crying for attention on a grand scale. The potential result? Sure, people may not objectify me as a pair of tits, but if I ever get as famous as I seem to desire, they'd see That Book Writer Chick before anything else, the magic of the moment of possibility gone forever.

And why in the world would I desire fame so much anyway? All of the people I knew before they were famous changed after they made it so big that they got recognized in public. Much like Eve Plumb, they seem just a little—scared. Of everything. All the time. It seems like a horrible life, really.

Okay, who am I kidding, if I could lose twenty pounds I'd love nothing more than to have people know me everywhere I go, maybe even have a camera follow me around all the time. So, if I can get a trainer then fine, I'll be famous. I could use the enormous wealth. I could earn a wealth so unmanageable I would have to use a company that specialized in Wealth Management Services. I could be so rich that I'll get one of those boyfriends like Kevin Federline, keep him on my payroll so he can dedicate every moment of his life to making me happy.

In fact, if, like Kevin Federline, my boyfriend has two children by his black baby-mama, I'll pay her child support rather than let my man have to go to work and take time away from his precious duties as Horse #3 on the draught team that pulls Jill, Inc., through the world each day.

Or even better than a horse and cart or a limo, I could be in the back of a van. I heard one of my favorite seventies has-been stars has a husband who drives her around in a big Astrovan, she in the back in some furry cocoon, probably on her cell. I imagine it chock-full of pink pillows, like the inside of Jeannie's bottle.

Come to think of it, now I realize why I fear the reality star more than the regular star. I must want to be the star of my own reality show. It will take place from the back of a pink van. It would be outfitted with fur and pillows, my boyfriend at the wheel. Most of the time I'd be splayed out, on my cell phone, giggling.

I wouldn't have to think of witty things to write into my computer, I would just be my witty self while the cameras rolled. And because it was all being broadcast, people wouldn't have to come up to the window to tell me what a beautiful toof I have, they could do it from the privacy of their own living rooms. I'd be a big special baby, with an endless parade of White Chocolate Dream Frappuccinos (in the big cup with the long green straw) standing by at all times. And all of you would have to watch. I'd be Ashlee Simpson but without the off-key lip-syncing. Ashlee Simpson who writes books, like Ashlee on a book tour, through the college towns of the Northeast. We can call it *Look at the Writer,* or maybe *A Medium-Sized Lady in Shiny Pants.* I'll let MTV—or better yet, Bravo—decide

3
Lotion Bag

"Look at yourself. You're perfect."

In the floor-to-ceiling mirrors that covered one wall of his bedroom, I could only look for a half of a flash of a moment.

What we were doing was illegal. I was seventeen and he was thirty-six and we had just had sex. But that's not why I couldn't look. I was running from the bathroom back to his bed, leaving slivers of myself everywhere: the girl who wanted to be here, the girl who didn't want to be here, the girl who thought the whole thing was exciting, that he was an idiot, that his apartment was tacky, yet sexy, that I was turned on, that I wasn't, that this was fun, that it wasn't. I couldn't look in the mirror because I would have been one person instead of a million, and that wouldn't have made any sense.

When I was seventeen, I had brand-new ginormous

breasts that had just arrived, sort of like Growing-up Skipper where you pull the arm down and they pop out. My skin was in shock—what are these? They probably looked like implants, hovering somewhere near my shoulders. The rest of me was miniature, so I'm guessing I looked like any man's version of a perfect woman. I say I guess as if I wasn't there, because I wasn't. Like almost all girls and women almost all of the time, if I looked at my entire body in the mirror, I was horrified. It was never right—even, it turns out, when it was perfect.

It was the summer after I graduated high school, before I went to college. Our family belonged to an urban version of a country club, called the East Bank Club. It had a rooftop pool and chaise lounges and Jewish women in white bikinis shading their eyes from the sun, yelling JESSICA! JEREMY! TIME TO GET OUT OF THE POOL AND HAVE A CHEESEBURGER! JOSHY! JENNIFER! I SAID NOW!

My sister and I spent our teenage summers at East Bank. Faith was a little tomboy jock, actually using the running track and lap pool. I was joined at the hip with Neille, and we looked really good together—she the ultimate Nordic blue-eyed blonde, me the exotic, curvy darkie, big brown eyes peeking out from my too-long bangs. At seventeen, Neille and I owned that rooftop deck, strutting around in our ripped half T-shirts (it was the eighties), string bikini bottoms, white socks and white Tretorns. When people would check us out, we'd give each other a haughty look that said "WHAT!!!???" as if they were being rude.

The Jewish moms would roll their eyes. Husbands would look up from their folded *Tribune*s a moment too long and get smacked by their wives. We had very busy days: back and forth from the chaise lounges to the bathroom to add blue eyeliner, to the Grill for salads, Banana Boat oil again, then into the water to cool off. Attract stares, sigh, reapply oil, bake, broast, attract stares, sigh, gloss the lips, barely eat, repeat, all day long, for an entire summer. We were finely tuned radios pointed straight to the attraction frequency.

I knew people had sex, but I didn't know the wide range of thoughts that went with looking at young girls and wanting to have sex. As far as I knew, sex was something two people did lying down, like an extension of hugging. If the two people get really really close, they might just get super-duper close by neatly placing the penis into the vagina. If you wanted to be incredibly dirty and have oral sex, you did 69, which was the same gentle naked hug, but upside down. Maybe it was the eighties, maybe it was my sheltered childhood, but there I was—the body of a centerfold, the mind of an eight-year-old. I was in no position to be consenting to anything, yet I was two months away from turning the legal consent age of eighteen.

There's consent, informed consent, and meaningful consent. Okay, I'm going to get academic[1] here, so bear with me. First of all, the age of consent is a misnomer. The law, as it is currently interpreted, actually allows all

---

[1] By academic I mean that I'm going to be using footnotes throughout, like this one.

people under eighteen to have all the sex they want—
with one another, and all people over eighteen to have
sex with one another, but never the twain shall meet.[2]
But I'm going to argue[3] that there are many, many
women of all ages who are not necessarily capable of informed, meaningful consent.

An erection is a very clear and hard thing; it stands
up and says YES. It goes in, moving like a missile toward its goal. The erection is necessary for intercourse to
occur. Strangely enough, there is no necessary desire-
dependent component for women.[4] Sure it helps if the
woman is lubricated, but it isn't a deal-breaker, physio-
logically, it's the weirdest decision God ever made. It
means that women can be raped and men can't, unless
asses are involved, and if you don't mind, I'd like to leave
asses out, at least for now.

[2]See Lindsay Lohan and Wilmer Vilderamma, as mentioned in *People* June 7,
2004. Lindsay and Wilmer were "just friends" until Lindsay's eighteenth birthday on July 28th, 2004, after which they were seen publicly enjoying affection
at both the Spider Club in Los Angeles, and the Sheraton Keilani on Maui.
[3]Are you wondering right now, Why are you arguing again, Jill? This isn't a book
for your college Womens' Studies class, this is a funny book with humorous personal essays, so save the arguments for another time. Here's the problem—I have
these theories that I need to share before I die. These may be my parting words.
I may be dead when you're reading this and you're getting the chills right now.
[4]Okay, now add in the stuff in chapter one where I talked about how only a
male orgasm is necessary for procreation! WHAT THE FUCK IS GOING ON?
AND WHY IS IT THAT THIS VERY IMPORTANT SCIENTIFIC TRU-
ISM—THAT ONLY MEN NOT WOMEN NEED DESIRE FOR SEX TO
OCCUR AND ONLY MEN NOT WOMEN NEED TO HAVE AN ORGASM
FOR LIFE TO BEGIN—IS BEING DISCUSSED FOR THE VERY FIRST
TIME OUTSIDE OF A SCIENCE BOOK. IN THE TEENY TINY PRINT
OF THE FOOTNOTE OF MY COMEDY BOOK? SOMEBODY HELP ME
UNDERSTAND THIS!!!!! NOW HERE ARE SOME QUESTIONS MARKS
FOR EMPHASIS?????????????

It means that a woman can think she's consenting but not be fully sure. It means that women can go back and forth many times in the course of an evening about what actually feels right or good or appropriate or safe, or wonderful or scary, but none of those things will affect whether or not the intercourse is *happening.* If a man loses interest, his erection flags and everything stops.

It is old news that in brain experiments, males depend more on the left side of the brain, which is in control of logic and material stuff, while more women have easier access to the right side, which is all, you know, abstract and flowy.[5] But what's fascinating is if you look at the way the brain neurons fire, on the left, alleged male side, they fire vertically, like a penis pole; on the right side, they fire horizontally, like the sea or a miraculous wind.[6] My aforementioned bleed-with-the-moon theory gives women the lock on time, while maleness corresponds with space, which involves rocketeering and jettisoning. My metaphors continue into orgasms: women's orgasms move in marvelous wet watery wide waves, while men's orgasms are marked by a unidirectional shot, often at the ceiling.

Thus,[7] women's desire lays itself out, wide and spacious, abstract. It waits, then accepts, it is the catcher. To truly, meaningfully, and conclusively consent may,

[5] Go look it up, I don't have time. I have a book to write, et al.
[6] My shrink, Joy Lowenthal, told me this. (She didn't say penis pole, I said penis pole. But she did say the stuff about the horizontal and vertical. I don't know if she's right, but I sure like how it supports my argument.)
[7] Isn't it fun when I say thus?

simply, not be synonymous with the nature of the equipment.

This brings me to my theory about the Kobe Bryant case. When it first happened I had an urge to call the news stations and tell them I was an expert, and that I would like to comment on what was going on.

My theory was that neither Kobe nor his unnamed accuser, whom I'll call Michelle, is lying. I think they were both there, in the same room, and would even testify that the same chain of events took place, yet they experienced it differently.

And when the case finally settled and Kobe made his statement, I felt vindicated.

"I recognize now that she did not and does not view this incident the same way I did. I now understand how she feels that she did not consent to this encounter."

This does not seem like a cop-out, nor a brushing aside of it all, but rather an opportunity for us to look at what happened and begin to speak about the fact that two people can be in the same room and experience something completely different. I can imagine exactly how it may have happened.

If Kobe is anything like most professional athletes, particularly those in Los Angeles, he must know all sorts of LA hoors[8] who are available at any moment. These are women who have not only watched porn but possibly appeared in a few, women who suck and fuck and bend over, then wipe up, squeegee out their holes, then go

---

[8] I don't use this term derogatorily.

downstairs and have a sandwich. Whether or not he had ever partaken of these LA chicks, Kobe might have thought young Michelle was just like them, that she wanted a taste of his big ol' chocolaty cock, here, there, or anywhere he felt like putting it. He may have even thought that the next day, they'd share a wave across the hideous, cranberry-colored fabric flowers in the lobby.

But Michelle might have had more of an Eagle, Colorado, Pop. 600, idea of sex. Michelle might have thought sex started with flirting, then conversation, a little kissing, then rubbing, perhaps rounding the bases of sexual progress, a dance of seduction.

Perhaps sex that night for Kobe was less of a dance and more of a drive-by. As I try to envision what may have gone on, I imagine that when Michelle got to his room, she probably got nothing like a kiss at all. Maybe from Kobe's point of view, they shared a dirty-talking quickie: suck it, get over here, I'm gonna cum in you, spank that ass, now go downstairs and get you a sandwich.

From Michelle's point of view, though, Things Turned Violent. Let's not forget that she was only nineteen—one to two years older than the age of consent in many states. At her age—probably without a whole lot of experience on which to base her expectations—her point of view may have been different: no foreplay, no making out, no seduction, just forcefulness and a one-minute bang that she wasn't even sure she'd consented to. Sure, by coming to his room, she had consented to something—but what? Did Kobe rape Michelle, or did Michelle just use bad judgment and end up having a short bad night of short bad sex?

The man who had illegal sex with me at seventeen was named Randall. He didn't hurt me. He was a Gentle Lover and an Elegant Gentleman, nothing but complimentary and kind, from the very first moment we met. It was a hot Sunday afternoon, and Neille and I were sitting at the Grill, nursing iced teas. A handsome man who looked like a more Jewish George Hamilton sat at the table next to us, his 14K golden *Chai* dangling on a fabulous flat serpentine chain.

"Hello there," he said, smiling modelly Pearly Drops teeth, "I'm Randall Golden." I opened my menu so I wouldn't have to endure yet another man hitting on Neille. Even though I was cute, when I was with Neille, I was invisible. I wasn't even Jill. I was just Not Neille. Randall slid his chair next to mine. I yawned and assumed the familiar role of insider buddy.

"Her name's Neille," I told him. "But she's very picky." I was sure that Randall would make one of the usual comments, à la "Neille, huh? You don't look like a boy!"

"Actually," he answered, "your friend is very lovely. But I'm more interested in you."

Sometimes in memoirs people fictionalize things. Sometimes people can't remember what was said, so they do their best approximation. But *Actually Your Friend Is Very Lovely But I'm More Interested in You* is EXACTLY WHAT HE SAID, word for word. I would swear my life on it. I had been plenty of people's second choices, and was always welcome to take the wingman of the guy who wanted Neille. And every so often, if Neille would walk away, a guy would focus his attention on me, ready to swing back when she returned. But here was a man, who was *giving up* his chance to woo Neille by saying this out loud, in front of her. I giggled and looked down and accused him of lying, of trying to use me to get to her. But he was dead serious and made it clear by asking me out for that very night. I gave him my address and we arranged a time that I'd be waiting outside my house.

The nausea at the core of the attraction/repulsion conundrum started. Did I want to do this? Did I not want to? Would it be fun or bad? Exciting? Safe? Scary? I concocted a lie to my parents that took literally no energy at all. Either they assumed I was adult enough to handle any situation or they were so embroiled in their own dramas that they didn't even notice when, at around seven that evening, I watched out the window for him, then said, casually, "Neille's outside, I'll be home in a few hours."

I ran out the door and into the black leather air-conditioned egg that was his Porsche 944.[9] The dashboard glowed with rich, creamery amberness. It smelled so fucking good, like wealthy people's new car, which is different from plain ol' new car. Good. It was good and good and air-conditioned and good.

As we drove down LaSalle Street and toward downtown, he pulled out a little black book. In it was a handwritten list of fabulous restaurants that would help him recall potential date destinations at the spur of the moment. Bad. This was really bad and bad and really bad,

---

[9] He also had vanity plates with his initials.

as queer as queer could be. My sister and Neille were suddenly crammed into the Porsche with me at that moment, pointing and laughing at his sad little list in his man-with-a-fountain-pen hand. I should have asked him to pull over right then, tell him I'd changed my mind, that it wasn't going to work. But I didn't know how to say that.[10]

I kept silent on his list. After all, maybe all 36-year-olds had lists, maybe that was just maturity. He chose a restaurant called Acorn on Oak. If you're from Chicago, you're laughing right now that this restaurant made it to his list. It was a dark little place with hamburgers and a piano. Randall sat back to the wall. I faced him. I could see the top half of my face in a mirror that ran the length of the wall behind him. The lights were low and my long bangs and overdone eyeliner were working for me. Over his beer and my 7-Up, I came clean and told him that I was seventeen, and not eighteen like I'd said earlier that day. He acted surprised, but assured me it was okay with him. He seemed enchanted by my personality. He was a trial lawyer and he thought I was smart. He said I had it all, I was beautiful *and* intelligent. He called me Supergirl. I knew what he wanted. I knew I was wanted. But I didn't know what *I* wanted.

---

[10] Have you noticed a theme? I've never known how to say anything remotely like "no" or "no thanks" or "I'd rather not." That would suggest healthy things like boundaries. Also, I've never known how to break up with anyone. As a youngster I either wrote long tedious letters in my roundy girlish hand, or had my sister call and pretend to be me. As I got older I wouldn't call back, avoided phone calls, or got caught cheating, then apologized, sobbing and snotting out of my nose, "I don't know what happened, I just don't!"

Sometimes there are those horrible rapes that get national coverage, like the mentally disabled girl in Glen Ridge or the girl in Los Angeles recently, both of whom were gang-raped. When these kinds of stories are in the news, the pain of the actuality of them comes at me like a snowball. I'll be driving down Wilshire Boulevard drinking a Frappuccino on my way to some fabulous movie meeting about some fabulous project when a chipper chick announces, "NEWS ON THE ONES AND WHEN IT BREAKS! IN THE ORANGE COUNTY GANG RAPE TRIAL, PROSECUTORS HAVE FOUND EVIDENCE OF A SECOND VIDEO TAPE INVOLVING FOOTAGE OF A MINI–BASEBALL BAT, MORE AT THE ONES. HEY! IT'S DOUBLE COUPON DAY AT VONS!!!!!!!!"[11]

At the center of all rape cases is the question of consent. But at the center of those particular cases is the idea of *informed* or *meaningful* consent. The prosecution has to prove that the rapists should have known that the alleged victim's consent wasn't meaningful, seeing as how, in these cases, the girl was mentally disabled or passed out cold drunk. Sometimes the prosecutors will argue that a woman who is mentally disabled or passed out drunk and the star of a home video consented, evidenced by the fact that people knew she was a slut, and

---

[11] Sometimes it's not what the news says, but that we have news, brutally equalizing all pieces into similarly sized soundbites in a row, like news sausage: gang rape, ten killed in Iraq, the Dow Jones is up two points. Just once I wish the announcer would catch her breath and say, "Whew. Wow. Now *that's* really sad," and then forget to say the thing about news on the ones, or Northridge Honda's tent sale.

besides, she went to a place where she knew what was expected of her.

This is what was argued about Kobe's Michelle. The prevailing idea was that (a) she went to his room and (b) she had sex with others, possibly the day before or after. This meant that she obviously liked sex, and simply, got some of what she liked. Sex.

From the non-informed consent of the video-taped gang-raped girl, to the not-meaningful consent of the mentally disabled Glenridge girl, to the hundreds of thousands of college girls who aren't sure whether or not they've been date raped—what none of these cases takes into consideration is the biological difference in the nature of consent. Because an erection is necessary for intercourse, male consent is implied. But the legal system often tries to prove that for a woman, once any door is opened—for example, once a woman goes to a man's room with the idea that sex is *possible*—consent is officially granted. Her rights are lost at the moment the door shuts.

For argument's sake, let's say a *man* opens the door to someone who said he was a door-to-door kitchen knife salesman. The salesman follows the man into the living room, but rather than display how to use the knives to slice tomatoes, he slices the man's throat. The victim would surely have a case and would gain much sympathy from a jury, even though he opened the door. The opening of the door would become moot, not a point of blame, as it became clear that the man who came in through the door misrepresented his intentions.

If Michelle went to Kobe's room and opened the door to the possibility of sex, what was she consenting to? Sex, or rough sex? Or any kind of sex that Kobe wanted? The court, by admitting into evidence the woman's sexual behavior of the past year, week, or day in leading up to the attack, showed its hand—that our legal system has an intrinsic bias against woman-owned sexuality. The defense's agenda became proving that Michelle liked sex or had sex with someone else the previous night. That was also the media's and our community's collective response to the situation. But if a man liked cooking and enjoyed great knives, his love of knives would not come into play when defending the murderer who disguised himself as a salesman. So why is it up for discussion here?

Moreover, why is the *nature* of the sex not admissible? As women who consent to sex, do we consent to *any* kind of sex, including violent and scary, every time we have sex? If this is the case, young women should know this. In all the talk about which one of these two was lying, or whether a girl who'd go to Kobe's room knew "what she was doing there," no one ever introduced the possibility that the nature of the sex might have *changed* from something Michelle desired into something she didn't. If Michelle was open to sex with a big black married man, then, as the courts and nearly everyone else saw it, Michelle was fair game for absolutely anything.

What if Michelle followed a traveling kitchen knife salesman to his room to see his wares, but thirty seconds later, he bilked her out of her money by charging her for a full set but never actually delivering them? Would she have a case? She would, in small claims court. What if he stabbed her with a knife, instead of a holy penis, or a super-holy penis belonging to a super-holy sports god?

Would she have a case? Indeed she would. What if Michelle followed a man to his room for satisfying love-making, but thirty seconds later, he held her down, smacked her, pulled her hair, fucked her in an uncomfortable way, way too hard, continued even when she said stop; would she have a case? It appears not. I wonder exactly what it is the law, as currently interpreted, would offer instead? To just feel yucky afterwards?

What if a girl met a man named Randall at a country club, and she had low self-esteem, because she was beautiful but not as beautiful as Neille, but he told her she was more beautiful, and so she went to his tacky fancy apartment, and he had sex with her, but she wasn't eighteen? Would she have a case? Or should she just feel yucky afterwards? Should Randall go to jail? Should he see Kobe there? Most important, if they ended up sharing a cell, would Kobe find succor in Randall's arms? Or would Kobe rock Randall into the shadowy night, both of them weeping?

After I had dinner at Acorn on Oak with Randall and we went back to his apartment, it wasn't with my consent. He didn't ask. He didn't need to. We were in his car.

Don't get scared. Nothing bad happened. Unless you consider boring sex bad. We went into his bedroom with the wall of mirrored closets, we made out, we had sex, he came, I pretended to. He bought my acting job with very little concern. I'm sure it was horrible, as I'd had nothing to base it on. I knew there was supposed to be some sort of build-up and release, but at seventeen, a really vigorous one—even faked—would have been way too embarrassing, so I'm sure I kept it quite petite and demure like a sigh, only sexier. The only remarkable things were that (a) he was somewhat not-well-endowed and used a variety of pillows to get us in workable positions, and (b) when it was all over, he got two towels very hot and wet in the bathroom and came back and placed them on my back in a relaxing fashion. That part with the hot towels was nice and something I'd recommend to everyone.

He didn't do anything mean or against my will. It was just strange and unfamiliar, the way a lot of sex is.[12] I continued to go out with him for the next few weeks, horribly faking a few more lame orgasms. I figured if the sex wasn't good, it was surely because I wasn't doing it right. And when I finally was ready to let it end, it had more to do with things that happened outside of his bedroom.

The first was that, when I asked him why he didn't go out with women his own age, he said, "Skeletons in their closets. Too many skeletons in their closets." It was the first time I had heard that phrase. But it scared me, because I knew one day I would be old and have skeletons. Of course, now that I am mature, I understand that he meant "Big-Dicked Skeletons."

The other thing that made me stop seeing him happened when we were on the rooftop pool deck lying on our chaises, dangling our fingertips together so he could get the Jewish moms gossiping and irate. Again, I knew I would be them one day, and I didn't know why he got

---

[12]Have you ever had a penis in your mouth and thought, "What in the hell am I doing? I have a penis in my mouth!"

a thrill out of watching them be jealous. I dropped his hand and changed positions, turning over. I put my arms behind my head.

"You're almost perfect," he said. Almost perfect? What the fuck? A few days before I had been perfect. I was Supergirl. He pointed to the stubble on my underarm. "You need to shave," he said. I looked at my underarms, horrified—it was maybe two or three days' growth. I dashed downstairs to the locker room and grabbed a blue plastic Bic from the Barbicide and ran it under my armpits. I ran back up to the pool and got in my chaise. My armpits were clean and fresh. But Randall and I were stale.

The next time I saw him at the club on the metal stairs between the racquetball courts and the arcade room, I made up a lie about having a new boyfriend. He took it like a man and wished me well, calling me Supergirl—and kissed me on the cheek like a father.

I didn't see much of him until late in the summer, just after Labor Day. Neille and I were on the sundeck, getting in our last few chances for just a soupçon more skin cancer. Faith had deigned to join us, probably because the ogling men she despised were gone for the most part. The pool was pretty empty, so we were surprised to see Randall strutting around at the far end, hovering near a sixteen-year-old with pale skin and straight red hair.

I turned over, hoping he wouldn't see me. But fuck, he saw us, and was headed our way. For some reason he still made me nervous, like a police officer or a judge. In a moment he was at the foot of our chaise lounges. We propped ourselves up on our elbows, shielding the late summer sun from our eyes. He was so tan, wood-brown. Only I was privy to the knowledge that up close, his tan was a collection of freckles, all run together.

"Have you seen my lotion bag?" he asked.

"Excuse me?" I said.

"My lotion bag," he said. "It's missing. My leather pouch? It's black and I keep my lotions in it."

We all looked at each other and shrugged. He fixed his George Hamilton eyes on us, all icy blue accusation. We hadn't stolen his lotion bag. But I wished we had. It was just the kind of thing we liked to do.

"No, haven't seen it," I said.

He huffed off, hands on his hips, tiny Jewish ass getting tinier as he headed back to the other side of the pool.

A millisecond passed. We were waiting, wondering, who would be the first. It was my sister. She said in the tiniest of voices,

"*Lotion Bag.*"

And we all just vomited laughing, hysterical, pounding the chaises trying to catch our breath. It was all that needed to be said. And for years after that, it was the name we would use to identify him: "I saw Lotion Bag today at Water Tower Place." And somehow, I knew that even if he was thirty-six and I was seventeen, even if I had sex with him when I wasn't even sure I wanted to, even if he had told me I had hair growing underneath my arms and that I was rapidly falling away from perfect, now that he was Lotion Bag, I had won.[13]

---

[13]the end

4

Monica, Chandra, and Me

Maybe you're not like me. Maybe you had a choice. If you're a Waspie or a Blondie or an Irish Catholic reddish freckled girl, or if you wore white to a ceremony as a child or walked down an aisle balancing a doily on your head, you had the opportunity to make a decision one day, whether to be bad, or to be good. When they looked at you, O Blondeness, they saw an angel. For you child, you were born pure. On the Madonna–Whore Game Show of life, you had a choice.

Jewish chicks, not so much with the choice. The typical conversation goes something like this:

Guy: Hey, you're pretty. Are you Italian?

Me: No, Jewish.

Guy: Oh, so you like sex.

No one had ever told me that women could do things like slap men or walk away. These women on television who throw drinks in people's faces are my heroes, seriously. I still want to throw a drink in someone's face before I die. Me, I'd either smile politely or look down and say, "Well, uh—," like the guy had pointed out that I was wearing a prescription shoe.

I'm always desperate for an evolutionary answer for everything. If I can just think of humans as a disease on the planet trying to breed, I can usually understand all I need to know. Maybe this is why Jews are so sexy. Because our genes are still in shock over the slaughter of half of our legacy, the code from our cell memory compels us to make more of us, as quickly as possible.

Additionally, this evolutionary excuse may account for intermarriage. Temple elders can complain all they want that so many of us marry outside of the tribe, but it makes perfect sense: If you want your genetics to move forward, *don't* be the thing that got so many of us killed not so long ago: Jewish. Interbreed. Mix with the ones no one hates, like the Swiss. In fact, as a matrilineally passed-down religion, Judaism was made for this, as long as the women do the intermarrying.

All of this adds up to my Why People Think Jewish Girls are Whores Equation:

(1) We have gargantuan insecurity around our identity. Our very first Jewish holiday memories include stories of people trying to steal our leavened bread or take our lamp oil or round us up and kill us since the beginning of time. In response, we've developed a bold need to propagate.

(2) We hold the knowledge that, secretly, we are the Best Ever, God's Favorite, anyway, because we're Chosen!

So ha ha, do whatever you want! Hell's for the goyim! This, I believe, creates a recipe for disaster: girls with large breasts who crave attention, have no fear of hell, and will do anything to avoid a train ride.

It is this equation that bred my tortured soul sister Monica Lewinsky, the Patron Saint of Jewish Whores. Monica truly got the really short end of the stick, never getting anything in return for her blow jobs—no cunnilingus, no intercourse. No nada. Just a bunch of really bad publicity. I really feel Monica deserves *something*. It can't be inconsequential like a muffin basket or anything you can order off the Internet. Something big. A parade or a musical tribute, at the least.

Or a statue. When I am president I will carve her out of ivory and place her in front of the Washington Monument, hanging naked and voluptuous and beautiful, not crucified, but Jewcified on a giant Star of David. When you get close to touch her, it will feel like she's covered in glistening donut sugar.

Before Kobe's Michelle, I wrote angry speeches in my head defending Monica. I wanted her to take the press conference stage in handcuffs (I know, there were no handcuffs, but let me have my story) and spit on the lenses of the news cameras, yelling, "Of course I blew the fucking president! You know how it feels to be a woman? Do you know how it feels to be told you will never be president, knowing you can *never* be the most powerful person in the world? Well at the moment I jiggled the president's balls in my left hand and stroked his shaft with my right, when Mr. Clinton leaned back to hold onto the door frame and steady himself as he moaned like a lamb, *I* was the most powerful person in the world!"

At the University of Wisconsin–Madison the Monica Lewinskys had their own sorority. It was called SDT, or Sigma Delta Tau. Everyone said SDT stood for Seldom Dated Twice or Start Diet Tomorrow. Oh, how we laughed and laughed at these brilliant word plays. As a freshman, I knew two things:

1) I had to be in a sorority if I wanted my college life to be fabulous like *Animal House* or *Porky's,* which was all I had to go on, and

2) I would not be in SDT.

My whole freshman posse was going through rush together—me plus my brand-new forty-five or so Best-Ever friends-for-life. Most of us were Jewish. The University of Wisconsin gave preference for in-state students for official campus dorms, and there was a housing shortage. Wisconsin produces about as many native Jews as it does palm trees, so the end result was a freshman year Minsk shtetl in a high-rise complex off campus, called The Towers.

Sorority rush came to Madison within the first week of college. Hey, here's a great idea. Take thousands of seventeen- and eighteen-year-old girls, on their own and living away from their parents for the first time in their lives. Put them in a group and then slowly but decisively, segregate them into smaller and smaller groups, showing them a list where utter strangers have rated them as Good Enough or Not Good Enough. A couple of days later, show them the list again, now adding the possible, You Were Good Enough Yesterday, But Now You're Not Anymore. Base everything on a one-minute once-over.

When all is said and done, in a Darwinist survival of the thinnest competition, the weak will be sobbing and begging to go home and work in their Dad's furniture store; the strongest will get pledge pins and begin a semester's worth of demeaning slave tasks, culminating in being publicly smeared with food. What a lovely way to begin anew, to cross the bridge from girl to woman.

Whoever decided this one was really thinking, and was probably responsible for creating *The Swan,* the only beauty pageant where you can start out putrid, undergo a year's worth of surgery in a weekend, and still be a loser.

The first night of sorority rush, we moved down the street together like a passel of Jewish scrubbing bubbles. As we walked to the student union to get split up into our pledge groups, we exchanged gossip: It was impossible to get into Tri-Delt if you weren't blond, wealthy, and beautiful. The two close behind were Alpha Phi, who were beautiful, blond, and had one tall half-Italian girl; and DG's, who were beautiful, blond, and may have had two girls with dark blond hair at some point in the seventies. The rest are just a blur that will only be recalled years from now in a hot saltwater bathtub during intense trauma hypnosis.

As we came down the street in our Forenzas and Famolares, carrying our rating cards like livestock, the sorority sisters stood betwixt the pillars of their big ugly goyishe greyishe houses, singing queerly and clapping. We stopped and listened and smiled. They really wanted us! They were telling us so in the lyrics of their songs! This was going to be a lot easier than I thought!

It seemed so simple: Just BE YOURSELF! they constantly told us, as if we even had selves yet. But it was nerve-wracking. I stared at my face in the mirror constantly, asking questions like, Am I cute enough? Do I need more Sun-In? and When will the diarrhea stop? I even got a wee little zit on my chin, something I had managed to get through all of high school without doing.

As the exciting days of the rush process progressed, I realized I was passing. I may have been a Jew but with my skinny little hips, huge, freshly baked breasts, and richy clothes from richy downtown Chicago, perhaps I appeared to be an asset. During the week of parties, it was my duty to carry a cup on a saucer (without spilling the tea), follow a girl whose name started with a K to a spot where I'd have to sit on a couch (without spilling the tea), carry on a two-minute conversation with K, stand (without spilling), and place the cup and saucer back down on a counter.

Against all odds, I carried it off. The only sorority I got cut from was Tri-Delts. I made it all the way down to the very last two second-best—but still really great, guys, I'm not lying—DG and Alpha Phi; and Alpha Phi really seemed to want me. I was finally going to ascend to my destiny—the token darkie in the hot (but keepin' it real compared to Tri-Delts) sorority. Soon that would be *me* standing on the steps, clapping and singing, my eyes filled with the kind of light you only get from having eighty-five best friends ever for life. Soon *I* would wear a light blue oversized sweatshirt with an A and an O with a line through it, grazing the ends of my royal blue and white-striped Dolphin shorts, demanding envy from all who passed.

A couple of days before the last party, the *sacred* party where we would see consecrated sorority things that could never ever be shared, we were hanging out in our suite looking at ourselves in the mirror, when I noticed my tiny zit was growing. By nightfall, it was huge and pus-filled and painful. I'd never had bad skin. I knew nothing about painful pus-filled zits. I'd seen other girls standing in the mirror and squeezing, so I tried it.

An hour later I had a face full of blood and a hole on my chin. No problem, I thought. I'll just cover it. We were all going out to some stupid bar to drink to traverse the very edges of our date-rape-ability that night, and I sure didn't want to miss that. I did the only sensible thing: blew dry my gaping wound with my hair dryer set on cool, dabbed in some concealer, powder, more concealer, and more powder to make a delightful spackling that I'm sure did a fine job. It was nighttime anyway.

The next morning when I awoke I had something where the zit had been that looked like a Volkswagen made of scabs. It was dark brown and crusty and oozing out something glowing and orangey from its very core. No problem, I thought as I peeled it all off and re-spackled, in order to look cute in case I saw a cute guy on my way to Food Science 134, which all the cute guys took. Even though it was now daylight, the spackle had to look better to the cute guys than the crusty wound, right?

But that night, when I got back to my room, it was clear I had a pretty big problem. The strength of the impetigo disease was threatening to outperform the disease that was Jill Soloway. I refused to contemplate my furture as a Seldom Dated Twice. I asked around about the rumor that I had another alternative—the news that another Jewish sorority was forming. Word had it there were some skinny Hebe girls with Jewfros, glasses, and opinions who needed to separate themselves from the lusty, busty SDTs. The AEPhi's were more like our other production-line prototype: Chandra Levy, the Patron Saint of Dead Jewish Whores.

Chandra, oh, my sweet sister Chandra. She didn't get anywhere near as much press as Monica but I loved her just the same. She was my sister, too. In 2000, when the news broke that she was missing, I knew she was dead and I wrote in my head for her as well, not angry speeches but mournful lullabies from the bottom of the river where I was sure she was waiting to be found. I was proved wrong when her remains were found in the park, but I was certain a ghost had dragged her body there.

I had watched those familiar Jewish parents on *Nightline* and *The Larry King Show:* Monica's proud, Hebress mother, Marcia Lewis, plus the honorable Dr. Lewinsky defending their daughter's right to blow the president. Now Chandra's distraught parents were taking the media stand, fiercely owning her, freely admitting their beautiful daughter may have had sex with grody Senator Gary Condit, but that didn't mean she deserved to die.

Gary Condit was no Bill Clinton, but he may as well have been. The attraction to tall gray-blond men with ties and the Dry Look hair is an undeniable one. Men like that are a Jewish girl's version of a challenge. They make laws or they chuckle or chortle, their shirts are pressed and possibly tucked into their saggy whities beneath their exclusionary Brooks Brothers pants. They nod and read sheafs of drafts of legislation; they are stern bosses and sensible managers. It is their ethos to remain strong and humorless, sort of like a flagpole. There is nothing more tempting than a flagpole to the crashingly violent sensual waves that are Jewish girls.

We need to see if we can take them down. We need to see if we are strong enough. We need to know why they can be president and rule the world, and we can't. We want to prove something to someone, holding our jizz-covered dresses up with the plea, But look! He loved me!

It was time to go to the last night of sorority rush. The Volkswagen on my face was now one of those plastic relief maps of the Western Hemisphere. I sanded and spackled for a few hours, then laid out my brand-new outfit: a gauzy white Esprit dress with tiny purple dots. I slipped it over my head, careful not to mess up my hair or my sculpture. If I stood this way, head tilted and to the left, it could pass for a townhouse development instead of a mountain range. I would keep my head down; after all, I was going to a sacred ceremony. Maybe no one would notice.

When I first got to the Alpha Phi house, everything seemed okay. No one was staring, and I was sure I would be fine if I could just stand in the corner and blot any errant leakage on a curtain. But then, there was an announcement. It was time go to the basement. Carrying candles.

My Rush Sis, whose name had to be Kim, handed me my candle. At the top of the stairs, we stood silently, hushed, respectful of the sacred ceremony-ness of it all. A girl whose name had to be Kristin handed Kim some matches. Kim turned to me. She struck the match, and it glowed bright with the secret fire knowledge that illumination is the heart of truth, and truth is beauty, and—

Kim lit the candle. I looked down at it, feigning sacred humility. I lowered the candle to as far away from my face as possible, but I could only get it as far as my arms were long, which wasn't anywhere near enough. The sound of something consecrated and Christian came floating up from the basement, and someone whose name had to be Kathleen told us to please pause for a moment.

I paused. Kim paused. Time and space and the very essence of the universe paused. But the truth of the light of the flame persevered. Something had to be known.

Kim looked at me, scrunched her tiny nose and said, "What's that thing on your face?"

"Huh? What?" I asked like I didn't have a clue what she was talking about. "Oh, this?" I pointed to my chin. "I don't know! It's just—I don't know! This weird thing, that, uh, I think I fell down or something."

"It is now time to enter the secret ceremony space. What goes on in our special basement must never be shared with anyone." It was the voice of KimKathleenKristin welcoming us into the ritual room. But I knew it was all over for me. As we stood in a circle and made promises in case we were chosen, I could see it all unfolding. That night, after we'd all left, the sisters of Alpha Phi would sit in the living room with their index cards. KatieKathrynKelly would say "Did anyone find out what that thing was on her face?" echoed by, "I thought she was cute until she came down here with that thing on her face," and a random "What *was* it?" Their voices would trail off and no one would even need to ask if I was a Yes or a No, it would be obvious. My card would be thrown on the floor, there would be a few giggles, and someone would say in a chipper voice, "Okay, moving on . . ."

The next day had a name like Bid Day but should have been called D-Day. We all were to go to the student union to find out which sorority wanted us. Anything could happen. We had written down our top two and they had written down their top two. There was also the terrifying possibility you could be crosscut, which was what happened if you picked ones that didn't want you. You would end up in no sorority at all.

As we walked over, stopping every few feet to vomit, we cheered each other on with the infinite optimism of the moments before things get posted on bulletin boards—test results, play auditions, class rankings. I could be anything, I could have an A or be Juliet or be number two, I could be anything!

I was nothing. Alpha Phi had rejected me. Okay, not nothing. I had one invitation to join a sorority. SDT. My sweet pudgy sisters, even though they had seen on my card that I wanted nothing to do with them, had invited me anyway. They welcomed me with their thick arms and tiny little sorority house on a street blocks away from the action. They wanted me. They saw beyond what was on my face.

But I couldn't accept their acceptance of me. I decided that the thing on my face was something important, some vital, smarter part of me, something deep inside me that literally bubbled up and told the world that I wasn't a sorority girl, even when I didn't know it myself. The Outsider Disease was stronger than the Cute Me Disease that wanted so badly to fit in, to get in. If left to my own devices, I would have joined Alpha Phi if they would have had me. But there was something else for me. It took awhile for me to learn that yes, I would have sisters, but I would find them standing on the outside.

In retrospect, I wish I would have joined SDT, or helped the skinny girls start AEPhi. I wonder who I would have been if I had. Now being Jewish is at the center of my identity, it informs everything I do. Seriously, I just did a word count and the word "Jew," "Jewish," or "Jewess" is in this story 267 times, the book 1,003.

The word "Jewess" describes who I am as much as the word "woman" or "writer." Jewess is my very own Nigga or Queer, a word invented by others to conjure someone bossy, frizzy, and demanding, but that I have reappropriated as prideful.

She is the part of me that wants to speak and needs to be heard, that floats to me on the wing of a dragonfly from a flower that blooms in the spot where Jennifer Levin was strangled in Central Park, or from a hummingbird who hovers above the place where the body of Chandra, whose name means "moon" in Sanskrit, was found in Rock Creek Park in Washington. It says a sisterly prayer for the life that would have been, or that could have been for Monica, and offers thanks to Marcia Lewis and Dr. Bernard Lewinksy, to Steven and Ellen Levin, for Robert and Susan Levy, and for Dr. Harry and Elaine Soloway, that your daughters' lives and careers and lost reputations have not been in vain. We are your offerings to the world, a world that has taken your leavened bread and stolen your oil, a world that tried to kill you and your parents and your grandparents; I write and they live and lived so that you might say to the world, take them, and let it be enough.

5

Please Don't Try to Kill Me After You Read This

The scary thing about writing a book is that it will be there forever. Even if actual paper books go out of fashion, my grandchildren will be able to drop in to their local fly-in space-library and auto-import a hologram of this onto their permanent chips. In the old days, you could be assured that your words would at some point be out of print, only found on dusty brown gluey pages at a garage sale. Not anymore. My concern is that, as terrific as all of this stuff seems to me today, it may not be so delightful to others. I see it as insistent and adorable. Some may not. When you write a book, you expose yourself to the reality that there are a lot of freaks out there, and a lot of them could even come after you if they don't like what you say.

But I'm brave.

I'm going to say it.

On the next page for dramatic effect.

I don't like dogs.

When we were little we had a cat, Pepper. I woke up from a dream that there was a cat in our yard and that morning, there was a cat in our yard. He decided to stay with us. He was the meanest kitten you ever met, and he grew into the meanest, fattest cat you ever met.

My dad hated Pepper. My sister and I think Pepper died when we were at college, but to this day I suspect my parents put him to sleep. No tears were shed. Pepper was an asshole.

At a few points later in my life, I got cats. None of them created a lasting memory. Nigel Von Sydow and I got a kitten but he made me name him Wombol after some British children's TV show that meant something to him and nothing to me. Perhaps because I didn't pick Wombol's name, I never really bonded to him. We gave him to a friend, who ended up losing him during a move. Tears, potentially, were shed, but they weren't mine.

But this isn't about cats. This is about dogs. Used to be, if I was forced to pick—cats or dogs, Pepsi or Coke, Mac or PC, my answers would be at the ready: cat, Coke, PC. But then one day, I was feeling a little loosey goosey, and it slipped out: "I'm just not a dog person." But you know, I'm going to go even further out on a limb. I've already said I don't like dogs. But watch this. Just watch it.

I hate dogs.

Yup. Go ahead, hate me. That's fine.

I do. I hate dogs.

Admitting this drives people *crazy*. People go nuts and then they wish to murder me. To dog owners, dog lovers, even regular people, it's worse than saying, I like Hitler.

People can't understand. Why? Why would I, a seemingly kind and decent person in every other respect of my life, a mother of a child even, a bringer of life even, hate dogs?

They smell like ham, for one. They lick everything and make your hands smell (like ham), and then you have to sidle your way over to the sink and wash your hands so the dog owner (whose hands smell like ham) doesn't notice that you're trying to wash the breath leavings of their beloved animal off of your hands.

Why do people have them? Why? Sure, on a farm, fine, on twenty acres or on a hunt, terrific. As an alarm system at your compound, fabulous, barking when someone pulls up in the driveway. But in your house? On your couches? In your beds, under the covers with you? Greasy animals, actual *animals,* with dander and triangular teeth and quills and ham-smell in your bed, where you sleep, in the nude? Or maybe you don't get to experience one of life's greatest pleasures, sleeping in the nude, because you have to wear pajamas to protect you from the many claws, the paws?

Paws, paw pads, leathery pads in five parts, black little pad thumbs? Scratchy black paw pads, and that one extra paw thumbnail hoofy thing at the back—why, people? Why is it there? It's called a dew toe! Why is it called a dew toe? To what end? Jumping, clawing, humping, knocking me down with their paws, attacking me, yes, *physically attacking* me when I enter a house?

Friends, if you had a brother who was in town visiting from Naples, and every time I came over he lunged at me and tried to knock me over, right down onto the ground, I probably would stop coming over. In fact, even if you said, "Oh, don't mind my brother, he's just excited to see you!" I would most likely not come back to your house until you told me your brother had returned to Naples.

Licking, slobbering, chopping, slobberchopping— pink gums, black gums. Which is it, is it pink or is it black? Sometimes it's both! Rubbery black lips, sometimes bumpy black lips, triangle canine teeth, pointy, pointy teeth, incisors everywhere, why? Scratching your legs, jumping, licking, stealing food at parties, jumping on me, jumping on my child. Why not just NOT HAVE them at all?

Come on, dog people, wouldn't your life be easier without going downstairs first thing in the morning, when you'd really rather pee but you can't because your dog's mooing, but then you get downstairs and find that the big ol' bowl of meaty, gravery kibble is surrounded by a trail of ants? Both to and fro? And why is there always fur in the water?

And why the barking, constant, constant barking, to wake your neighbors, or me at six in the morning, and again at six-fifteen and six-eighteen and seven and eight and nine? To say nothing of the yapping during my precious, precious nap time, or TV time? And do you know, do you have any idea, that the moment you leave for work, your dog starts barking and doesn't stop until you return? Did you know this? WELL, NOW YOU DO, DOG PEOPLE! YOUR DOG BARKS WHENEVER YOU AREN'T THERE!

Additionally, I continue, if you are a dog owner and have any kind of gathering, you either have to hide the food or put the food on a special table fifteen feet high and keep telling people not to let the dog near the guacamole or the chocolate. Then a piece of brownie or an errant avocado-smeared Tostito hits the floor and the dog eats it, but no one's noticed because everyone's gone outside for a few minutes because the groom's friend from Ottawa wants to make a toast, and by the time everyone comes back in, the entire table has been cleared and is on the floor and the dog is tasting everything with his mouth that has just been in another dog's ass.

Then the owner tries to salvage a few pierogi, but we know they have dog ass on them. Then the dog vomits and the owner tries to drug the dog with syrup of Ipecac or Benadryl to make it go lie down in the TV room so a few people can continue to try to have a nice time, even though the pierogi is ruined. And then sometimes, if Aunt Lily's glasses case gets chewed up with Aunt Lily's glasses in it, the owner has to offer to put the dog to sleep, just to appease Aunt Lily; and so I ask you, why not just not have them?

The walks, the constant walking, having to leave the house before sunrise and after dinner, during TV prime time, then walk for miles and miles around the neighborhood, forced into conversation with other tedious people who feel they know you just because you both like getting dragged around the block nightly by hounds; the leashing, the tagging, the ordering of the tags from the tacky catalog that also has the mono-grammed pillowcases and return address labels with clowns on them, the changing of the tags every time you move, the running away, the returning to the old house, even if it's a thousand miles away, the losing, the find-ing, the dragging back home by the scruff of the neck, the ham smell, the ham smell, the ham smell.

Oh, and just so you know, if you're a guy, there is nothing less sexy than seeing you coming toward me walking down the street swinging a plastic bag full of shit. I know what you're saying right now if you're a dog lover, you're saying you don't care if I think you're sexy or not, because if I don't like dogs I don't exist. WHAT-EVER!

I also can't stand when your dog comes running up to me and tries to fuck me with its nose. It's as if your pooch wants the world to know I have a stanky-ass pussy. That's what they're saying! Not to me, of course, I mean to say that's what it implies to *one,* when a dog ap-proaches one's down-there, as Lisa Latkin used to call it in sixth grade. Me, *my* down-there smells like peaches and Calvin Klein's Obsession.

Okay, to be fair, I must admit—there is one thing I like about dogs. This is a fabulous secret and I only hope that by writing this in this here book I'm not ruining it. Dogs are a wide-open window into their owners' feelings. Dog owners will admit truths and betray themselves, revealing their hearts' desires over and over again, if you just pay attention to the way they speak to and about their dogs.

The first time I noticed this was when my son and I were visiting my mom in Chicago. She had a golden retriever named Sasha. I knew for sure that Sasha was a great window into my mother's unconscious when we were all in the living room and my mom looked Sasha in the snout and said, "What's wrong baby? Too many people in the house? You having a hard time with all the people the people the people all the time? Don't worry, they're all going back to LA soon, and you'll be able to get back to your routines. Yes, yes, that's a good girl. Yes you do love your routines, you do you do!" It occurred to me that maybe it was my mom who loved her routines (she does, in fact) and that she was just saying it was true of Sasha to feel like they were both members of a routine-loving club, perhaps named The Routine Lovers.

After this, I started noticing that strangely, everyone's descriptions of their dogs could easily be a description of themselves. Por ejemplo: I once answered an ad in the newspaper for a car for sale. The guy who answered the door was a hippy-dippy dude in tye-dye and overalls with a German shepherd mix panting at his side. He told me not to worry, that his dog was on the "super positive energy tip." What a coincidence, I thought, that this fellow's dog doesn't love routines!

A very insecure, low-self-esteem man I dated—so much so that at bedtime, he would take a shower and then put on deodorant for sleeping—repeated over and over to his dog, "Awwwww, you think nobody loves you. You poor thing, you think nobody nobody loves little old you." And even just the full-on admission, "Nobody loves you do they? No one at all, widdow one, no one at all loves you."

A supersexual friend of mine, a wacky chick who even had proudly dabbled in light prostitution at one time in her life, used to lie on the bed with her dog, rub the dog's tummy, and tell her "Who's a sexy girl!? You are! You horny, horny girl, you're such a sexy little slut dog! Aren't you just a slutty little slut girl?"

I could go on and on. A friend of mine who takes loads of medication for her obsessive-compulsive disorder describes her dog as "a neurotic mess." Okay, actually I can't go on and on. That was my last one. I was going to make some up, but I know that you're thinking about all the dog people in your life and having a laugh right now, so I'll let you do so.

Are you back? Have you thought about everyone in your life and all the things you now know about them? Good. Because I need you to know something else. While I was writing this, it occurred to me that if people are projecting what they believe about themselves through their opinion of their dogs—and I hate dogs, all dogs—what does that mean for me? Do I hate humanity? Do I hate being human? Do I hate life, in its many forms? Is it women I despise? Jews? MYSELF?????

I didn't want this to be so. Upon rereading my diatribe, I could see my problem. I was lacking some deep, important ability to connect with my own soul. If it's true that dogs want nothing more than to please their owners, and that for most people, dogs provide an expression of their owners' inner worlds, perhaps it was their very reflective-ness that I hated. Perhaps it was seeing myself that I feared.

I decided to keep my eye out for dogs I could actually like. I started talking to dog owners and smiling, averting my eyes from their shit bags. A few people walking past had dogs that I stopped and petted. There's a chocolate lab named Chico that always stops for a neck scratching, and a little white mutt named Augie that yips in a way that isn't incredibly annoying.

But everything really changed a few weeks ago when I saw Mika. She was the most stunning, blond, soft, clean, stately, gorgeous Akita. Her owner kept her on a tight leash every day as they passed our house. Sometimes, when I was getting in my car, I'd see her and she'd look at me and I'd look at her. Then, one day, I felt a magical feeling that told me to go outside for a barefoot walk. When I came down my steps, Mika and her owner were there.

"Can I pet her?" I asked.

Her owner brought her over to me, loosening the choke chain by one knuckle's worth. I crouched down. Mika came right to me, and we put our foreheads together. We rubbed cheeks. We nuzzled. She smelled so good. I didn't care that her gums were black and rubbery, I wanted to make out with her. I love this dog, I thought. I want this dog. This is my dog. I looked up.

"She's so beautiful," I said to her owner. "Where did you get her?"

He told me the story of a man down the street who had died and left Mika to him.

"*We're* looking for a dog," I said, for no good reason. "If you ever need to find another home for her, please let us know."

"Everyone wants her. Everywhere I go people say they want her," he said.

"I can see why," I replied. He yanked on Mika's chain a little, signaling that it was time for us to let go of one another's souls. But it was hard to let go. I felt like I'd finally found my dog. I could love this dog. Forever. I looked her in the eyes and whispered, "Mika, such a pretty, pretty girl, and such a good girl. And nobody knows it, do they? But you're really such a good girl, aren't you?" I asked.

Mika nodded, and followed her owner away. I walked down the hill, barefoot and magical, and trying my hardest not to think about all the work I would have to do when I got back home from my walk.

6

Found My Way in LA

Los Angeles is Magic. It's yellow-orange-red and the smog makes everything blurry in a good way. I hate when people come to Los Angeles and just bitch, bitch bitch. I know it's not New York. I know it's not Chicago. Yes, some of the people here are fake. Shut up and go home. I love landing here. When I emerge into the sun at LAX after I've been away, I hear Joni Mitchell singing her song.

> *Oh, but California*
> *California I'm coming home*
> *I'm going to see the folks I dig*
> *I'll even kiss a sunset pig*
> *California I'm coming home*

When I visit other cities, I go out of my way to praise them in a fake high voice. "Wow, Chicago is getting so cosmopolitan!" and "Hey! Boston has some great shops!" When people come here, they're not five minutes on the ride in from the airport before they say flatly from the back of their throat, "I could never live here."

I really don't care if you could ever live here. Magic happens here and maybe you just can't handle the magic. It's not wiggly Marshall Brodien magic with hats and bunnies, or new age majick with chakras and the moon. This is just Los Angeles and it's in another color than most cities. You just have to put on your sunglasses so you can see the colors.

Los Angeles is the color of dreams. The city is filled with people dreaming, people who escaped. The special people, the people too beautiful for their towns or too weird for their high schools. Yes, many of them eventually end up dressed up as Superheroes charging a buck a picture on Hollywood Boulevard, but at least they had dreams once.

Most people are stoned, on either weed, Xanax, or yoga. We're so close to Mexico that people drive slow without knowing it. LA is Spain and Compton and a desert salt flat braided into one thing. It's a Hummer with blaring Chingy as a little Guatemalan man walks by with his cart, ringing a bell to sell an ear of corn covered in Parkay and paprika. Silver Lake and Echo Park are fuck-yous to what the Lower East Side has turned into. Race down Sunset on a Sunday to Beverly Hills where you can walk through Brighton and Camden and be eye to eye with seventy-year-old women with puppies and tight jeans and white slings on their faces, fresh from Dr. Birnbaum. There are mountains and skid row and Malibu and gay town, Armenians and Thai Town all in one neighborhood and high school gang bangers with magic markers instead of spray paint, I love it here. The only thing you have to get used to, is that it's . . . wide, I guess.

If Los Angeles was stacked all on top of itself, New Yorkers would get it. But it's not, it's dribbled across too many miles, horizontal in the feminine way I like things to be, long and flat, not tall and phallic. If you zoom from appointment to appointment in your car listening to *Morning Becomes Eclectic* on KCRW, you feel it. You pass through your LA vortex, let the warm weather and pink mountains and Elliot Smith smooth you, let the sunsets you can count on melt the blue icicles from your long winters. And don't worry, you can still be sad here, even if your icicles are melted. Smog is like rain. It's fun to be sad in LA.

I traveled through my vortex all in one day, about six months after I got here. I had just started working on a new job. In the morning, on the way to work, I stopped at the bank to get a roll of quarters for parking meters and walked past the front. I made eye contact with the security guard, this sweet older fellow with sandy John Denver hair. You only find old guys like this in LA, still trying to pass themselves off as blond, as if we don't notice the silver roots and leathered skin and coke bottle horn-rims. But he was a sweet old guy, and I always said hello to him, and he always nodded, rocking on his heels and stalwart, ever on the lookout for trouble.

As I waited in the teller line, I started thinking about him, wondering about where he lived and what his apartment looked like. Was it small? Just one room? Did he cook on a hot plate? Did he know his hair looked like a wig?

Maybe it *was* a wig. Maybe he had cancer and chemo and the bank only gave him his job back because he needed something to do or he'd die of boredom, and they didn't want *that* on their hands. Or maybe he begged to get his job back, because the health insurance paid for the last few chemo treatments. He really did look very tired. God, what a horrible circle, his life: standing in the bank to pay for the chemo to keep him alive so he can stand in the bank to pay for the chemo to—

I got my roll of quarters and stopped to get the bathroom key. The bathroom was behind the security guard, and when I passed behind him, I saw that he had something in a drawer, attached to a very taut nylon string. This must be where his gun is, in the drawer.

Now this was really sad. They give him a weapon, but he has to keep it in a drawer. Maybe he's so bad with weaponry that he needs to get a supervisor's approval, like at Ralphs when you get your check approved. Poor guy actually needed a supervisor's okay to get his weapon out. Would there be enough time in a bank robbery? Did they really feel confident he could do his job well, needing a person to bring a key to get to his gun?

I looked closer and noticed that he appeared to be attached to the string and that the string was attached to the drawer. Now *that* was really sad. They keep him chained up here. Maybe he couldn't even leave or go to the bathroom without someone else's approval. God, it broke my heart. What a job, a security guard. But one who can't move, who is literally a prisoner, just to keep all of us safe while we do our banking.

When I came out of the bathroom I looked one more time. This time I noticed something else about him.

I noticed he wasn't real.

He was made of wax.

He was a dummy, a wax dummy in a security guard uniform.

I had questions, so many questions. Did the one I know die to be replaced by a dummy? Or has he always been a dummy? But I've smiled at him, I've said hello to him for the past six months, he's nodded and smiled at me.

"Oh my god," I said. The two big black human security guards just chuckled.

I went to my car.

Everything that looks like something can change in one day, by moving your vision one percent. I looked one percent harder than I normally do, and I saw that string. Still, I was unable to believe he wasn't alive.

If a judge had asked me before that day to swear on my life and my son's life and everyone's life, I would have said that was an absurd question and of course, the security guard in the lobby of the City National Bank was alive.

At work that day, I found out that my whole life I had been spelling "simultaneous" wrong. My entire life.

That afternoon I was leaving work, CBS Radford in Studio City. I was in my car, waiting at the light at Colfax and Ventura, right next to Killer Shrimp. My passenger door opened and a beautiful young girl got in. She looked at me and said, "Hi."

"Hi," I answered.

"Can I come with you?" she asked.

"Okay," I said.

I thought maybe she was in trouble, that an abusive boyfriend was following her. She was so young and cute and white and pretty that I wasn't scared, not at all, just worried for her safety.

"Um, is everything okay?" I asked gently. She smiled and nodded. She seemed calm for someone who had just taken a seat in someone else's car. Maybe she was having some kind of bipolar break and she needed me to drive her home or to her mom's or to a phone where she could call her psychiatrist. Maybe god had put me in her path so that she wouldn't get attacked by some freak who didn't have the same compassion as I did.

"What do you want?" I asked her.

Why did I ask her that? What do you want? What kind of a question was that? Was I as crazy as she was?

Dramatically, she whirled and looked straight at me, her eyes wild. "I want to be famous and I don't want to go to school!" she said, hysterical. The light turned green. She looked at me and smiled again.

"Take a left." I did. She pointed to white pickup truck in front of her.

"Follow that car." Aha, I thought. A clue. The abusive boyfriend. Someone to make it all make sense. I took a left on Ventura and followed. But the white pickup took a left into a muddy abandoned parking lot worksite-type thing. I looked at her as if to ask, "You seriously want me to follow a pickup truck into an empty

parking lot at night? Are you off of your crankin'
crank?"

As if to ask. I didn't ask. I was under her spell. As
you know, I have a boundary problem I've been carping
about. I said nothing, I just looked at her. She knew
what I was thinking, I guess.

"It's okay," she said. Still employing my horrible
judgment, I did just what she said. I imagined the sce-
nario unfolding. This was their scam. Her junkie
boyfriend probably made her get into women's cars and
appear vulnerable, then direct them to the parking lot
for some robbin' and rapin'. What the hell was I thinking? And how was I going to get out of this?

I pulled into the lot. The white pickup truck did a
U-turn and faced the road. I pulled up next to the driver,
driver's side to driver's side.

It was a man. He rolled down his window.

"It's my father," she said.

It was. He was about fifty and Armenian-looking.
He was very calm for a man whose daughter was in a
stranger's car. He looked at her and sighed.

"What do you want to do?" he asked.

"I wanna be an actress, *and I don't want to go to
college!*" she said.

"So what are you gonna do?" he asked.

"I don't know!" she said. She looked into my eyes
for an answer. Did she think I could tell her she should
be an actress? I *was* a TV writer, after all. I guess I could
try to get her an audition for a voice-over on the cartoon
I was working on. Maybe that's why I was in her path,

maybe a young Angelina Jolie was sitting right here in my car and I, the Hollywood producer, would be her mentor, her shepherd, get 10 percent. Instead of saying all of this, I just shrugged.

She looked at her dad, then at me. Her dad pulled out a cigarette and lit it.

"Could I have a drag?" she asked.

"No," he said.

Another few moments passed. He blew smoke out his nose and stretched out his neck.

"Get out of her car," he finally said. She looked at me again and smiled.

"Thank you," she said. She got out of my car and into his.

"Thank you," her dad said to me, then pulled it into drive and rumbled off.

That night I went to dinner with a few friends, a whole bunch of the people I dig, Chicago friends. When Joni says she's going to see the folks she digs, I'm right there with her. All of my really close friends are here, including one of my oldest and bestest friends, Wayne. Wayne brought with him this friend from work; I can't even remember her name. She had blond hair, nothing special, just this girl you'd never even notice.

We were having a lovely evening. I believe baked ziti was involved. I told everyone my story about the pickup truck, and they laughed at my imitation of the teenage girl's hysteria. But I didn't even remember to tell my wax security guard story, because about halfway through dinner, I started staring at Wayne's friend's face.

I started to obsess on her nose and her mouth, and the way her nose connected to her mouth, and suddenly I was captured by the thought that she was exceedingly ugly. Everyone was busy eating baked cheese-covered dishes and chatting, and I was busy eating baked cheese-covered something, but I couldn't stop staring at her nostrils. I hated the way they looked like perfect, tiny hearts. Her chin was too small. And her eyes drove me crazy. The distance between them was just so pedestrian. The only way to describe her face was to call it aggressively boring. I couldn't get the thought out of my head that this girl was the single most ugly person I had ever come across in my life.

That thought obsessed me for the rest of the dinner, and I was relieved when it was finally over and I could stop thinking about how incredibly, annoyingly ugly she was. As we stood in the foyer and said our good-byes, Wayne's friend went to the bathroom and Wayne pulled me aside.

"Did you like her?" he asked.

"Sure," I said.

"Oh, good," he said. "I am so glad you finally got to meet her, Jill. I've always thought you two looked exactly alike."

I hugged Wayne and went back to my car and went home to my studio apartment with the yellow walls with big saffron diamonds painted on them. And the next day, when I got up for work, I forgot to wonder what I was doing here. I just made my coffee, took a shower, kissed my sunset pig, and headed out the door.

7

Jill of Finland

Believe it or not, Neille—my blond companion and rooftop-deck partner in crime—and I are still best friends. After high school, she went to art school while I was in Madison, and we kept in close contact the whole time. I'd either return to Chicago to visit or she would come up to Wisconsin for a weekend. We shared the exact same sense of humor, some of the same guys, and a really bad case of crabs. Neille eventually upended everyone's expectations that she would marry really, really well, and instead, held onto her singleness and started her own mosaic table empire, making scads of money.

When we were in our early thirties, Neille moved to LA. We took up our old ways of going out on the town together to do our favorite show, the snappily sexy Blond/Brown Sandwich. In Chicago, when we would hit the Rush Street bars in my mom's rabbit jackets, we were seventeen pretending to be thirty-three. Now in LA, we were thirty-three pretending to be seventeen.

Neille is not a Jewess, but you would think she was if you heard her on the phone. If Jewish women really do have extra testosterone like I've heard, then she's one of us. Neither of us can relate to letting a man feel smart so that he can feel more masculine. If a guy says something stupid, you have to point it out.

She and I had traveled much the same path, being fabulous and beautiful and wondering why guy after guy after guy was never good enough for us. We ended up taking on the same shape in life, a shape some might call macho, but because we're women, I'll call eggo. We were both unbelievably driven to be successful, sadly aware that to make guys find us attractive we had to shut our ever lovin' mouths, even for a few minutes. We really did much better trolling for men on our own. When together, we would eat guys alive, more interested in making each other laugh than making progress.

Some guys were into my big-mouthed bossy side. It was not uncommon for me to begin a relationship with a guy who had been super-duper interested in me, only to find that when we got to sex, he wanted me to dominate him. For a couple-year span, guy after guy after guy would whisper to me in the dark, sheepishly, that he would get off more if I would take control. Anything I wanted would be fine, anything at all, spanking, bossing, standing on them in my street shoes. They'd lie prone, eyes closed, and thighs twitching, waiting for whatever punishment I chose to dole out.

Sure, I guess it's obvious to you that I come off as a know-it-all, Bossy Boots on Fire, but inside, I was a gentle flower and couldn't figure out why this kept happening. I had no desire to violate anyone. If forced to choose, I'd rather let someone else do the bossing. It's much less work to just follow orders, do what the nice man says. Like being drunk or high for sex, it's yet another way to conveniently rid yourself of the responsibility and the contiguous, fun-squashing shame.

In fact, to return to my lecturing about gender and consent, just when you'd hoped I was finished, it has always seemed to me that a certain percentage of date rape cases are ultimately about class. White educated upper-middle-class people who read *Harper's* are very comfortable having a pre-sex conversation negotiating a power dynamic. They know a top from their bottom and they've read their erotica collections. Like their brunch, they feel no guilt about ordering up their sex platter with very specific needs—egg whites only, wheat toast no butter, I'm gonna need you to squeeze my balls really really hard right before I come.

Do date-rapers know they could find plenty of women willing to consent to their dom fantasies, and, with a little imagination and polite negotiation, be as turned on as they want to be and not have to run the risk of going to jail? As long as it is within the confines of a caring, safe relationship, many women like thinking about being taken while they're having sex. In college I asked my friends if it was easy or hard for them to have orgasms, but never asked anyone exactly what *made* them orgasm. But now, when the topic comes up, I ask as many women as will let me: What do you think about when you come?

A huge percentage share that, whether they're masturbating or with a partner, they like to think about being objectified (everything I ever took a stand against) or imagine it's all happening against their will (everything every woman ever worries about). Did this evolve as a response to us always being objectified anyway? Would we fantasize about having our spirit cared for through lovemaking if this was the norm? Or do I just happen to know a lot of people who are writers and actors, weighting my sample toward women who never got enough attention as children and evolved into fetishizing it during sex?

Boy, I think a lot, don't I? No wonder everything's so hard for me. "Jill, you think too much" has been said on many an occasion. I really don't like when people say that, mainly because it's always a man, and it usually means "Shut up and start suckin'."

In trying to escape this spinning in my skull, I tried some unexpected things. For a few solid years, I was high as a kite on marijuana. God, I love me some marijuana. I almost never do it anymore—I'm too old and I have way too much work to do and I always come down with a cold a couple days after I try it. But for a while there, it was the only thing that would shut off this ticker clicker clacker in my brain and let me have what I'd heard people talk about—this thing called "a good time."

I also found that I could relax my gears if I dated a

certain kind of man—not Jewish. Maybe I'm too competitive. Maybe I'm too much like their mothers. Maybe I came of age during the wrong time—while Philip Roth and Woody Allen were authoring the shiksa fetishizing trend. Around the same cultural moment, Neil Simon wrote the movie *The Heartbreak Kid,* about a Jewish man whose annoying wife got so sunburned on their honeymoon that she had to hole up in a hotel room so he could lust after Cybil Shepard. In a strangely self-hating move, this was directed by Elaine May, a Jewish woman herself. Yes, Jewish men *and* women helped advertise the idea of the worthless Jewish wife. They taught Jewish men how to hate us, and taught us how to feel hated. And it worked.

By the way, the tide is turning in this area. I predict a move away from the thin blonde withholding ideal and a tilt toward the warm, mushy brunette. It could be temporary, a result of 9/11, the social trend they call "cocooning"—a wish for nurturing protection—but I believe certain new movies might bode well for my kinda lady.

James L. Brooks (who has had more power in my life than God, and who may in fact actually be the Jewish God) has, with the recent release of *Spanglish,* is perhaps turning the tide. Watching it made me think Brooks is sick of the hyper-exercised blond Tea Leoni and wants to go back to his roots, comfying up under the covers with a real live Jewess. Okay, they would never do that, but a real live Jewess in the costume of the dark and sultry Latina maid, with her bosomy maternalism and warm instinctual ways. Playing for the Latina-Jewy Darkies, we have a kick-ass starting line up: Penelope Cruz, Salma Hayek, Eva Mendes, Paz Vega, Natalie Portman, Jennifer Connelly, and Rachel Weisz.

Unfortuantely, this trend is shaping up is a little too late for me. When I was young, there was nothing more reviled by Jewish men than . . . me. A lot of Jewish men didn't even bother hiding the fact that they never went out with Jewish women. In fact, they waved it as a point of pride. First there were the Jewish men who only dated Asian women. This drove me so crazy that I contemplated a stand-up act that centered on my hatred of all Asian women (except Margaret Cho). That was going to be part of the hilarity—saying "except Margaret Cho" à la Seinfeld's over-repeated "not that there's anything wrong with that," way too many times.

But I really did have a lot of anger toward Asian women. I felt they did white women a disservice. I despised the way they sylphed around town in their tiny, hairless bodies, turning up on the arms of the funniest Jewish comedy guys, guys who were *my* birthright. I called them girlcats, like they were a mixed breed, somewhere between females and Siamese cats. I scowled when Jewish boys I knew shrugged, saying, "I don't know what it is, their pussies just taste . . . really, really good." I couldn't stand that their "otherness" turned guys on, because I knew that what they were "other" than was me.

Soon the Asian fetish went out of fashion and was replaced by the winners of the Porno-ization of America pageant. I just can't compete with these women—maybe that's why I'm trying to stamp them out of existence.

They're like Dick Candy. They really and truly look like they've preened and primed themselves, those nails and those giggles and that newscaster-Yuko-system hair, just to look as good as possible—at the end of someone's penis.

When Neille moved here from Chicago, we complained endlessly about the proliferation of the Dick Candy. We would go out at night to Sunset Boulevard, the center of the action in LA. But as 5'4" thirtyish chicks who had gained a pound a year since high school, we looked like square linebackers in heels compared to the newly arrived homecoming queens from every state in the country. We were competing with seventeen-year-olds with fake IDs. Oh my god, it was us fifteen years ago. No wonder all those people gave us such dirty looks back in the day. Eventually we gave up trying to find whoever He was and started staying in, cozying up in my Echo Park apartment, eating big bowls of cereal and watching TV to kill the pain.

One night Neille and I decided to run down to the local corner tavern for a beer. Just a beer, no trolling, no looking for The One. There was a place without a sign that was even in walking distance, and I suggested we go in and get a little ungentrified local color. We figured no one would be inside except a couple of toothless homeless people. But when we got there, there was a huge line of double-long, double-high shiny black pickup trucks snaking around the block. Hmm.

The sound of Springsteen pumping inside leached out. I opened the door to a vestibule where a storm of

Paco Rabanne and Marlboro Red smoke came whooshing at us. This was weird. Smoking wasn't legal indoors in LA anymore. What kind of bar would let so many patrons do something so illegal?

A cop bar. Frankly, at first we thought we'd walked into a gay leather bar. The place looked like one of those Tom of Finland drawings. He's that artist you find next to rainbow stickers in gay stores—tacky sketched pencil portraits of mustachioed men in captain caps with ham-hock thighs. Everywhere we looked there were men with gigantic arms and stern eyes, leaning against wood paneling, downing beers. Some were unstrapping giant pistols and putting them away in gun lockers for safekeeping. We had happened upon a night called Payday Wednesday at a bar called The Short Stop. It was the LAPD's twice-monthly celebration, where, after they had just been handed their government-issue checks at work, they were ready to let their regulation-length hair down and dance dorkily.

As I walked through, I finally knew what it felt like to be Heidi Klum. The men stared, every last one of them, heads turning in rhythm to "Dirty Ol' Town." Coincidentally, this bar was also on Sunset Boulevard, but it was planets away from the scene down near the Marmont and the Mondrian and the Dick Candy. These guys were used to tired-out biker chicks with halter tops and crow's feet in their cleavage. The Short Stop was what I called "win-win" at its best.

Neille and I looked at each other, checking if it was possible we were so connected by now that we actually dreamed together. This place rocked. There were two hundred men and us, and we were the queens of the world again. The cops knew how to flirt. Bossy by trade, they simply struck up conversations as they handed us drinks, without even asking if they could buy us one first. Their manliness reawakened my dainty feminine sparkle. My urge to chop guys off at the legs was gone.

I was high, floating through the contingents that staked out sections along the bar: the stocky farm boys from Oklahoma, new to LA and full a' piss; the brown-skinned third-generation Latin guys with names like Soto and Martinez; and my favorites—the badass Metro cops—Aryan, icey-eyed older guys who looked like they talked dirty in their sleep.

Neille and I had found our very own tit bar (the cool new name for titty bar, which used to be the cool new name for strip club). But this place was so *not* Chippendales. No guys named Darius, oiled in coconut and swinging that sack of genitals in a circular fashion. Anyone who ever suggested that women could combat sexism by going to male strip clubs is a complete idiot and doesn't understand anything about everything. Men shouldn't do that silly booty quake thing where their buttocks go back and forth really fast like jello. Men need to stand still and fold their arms, barely move. And that's exactly what the men in the cop bar did.

Just as female strippers seem like tragic, exaggerated versions of femininity, the cops were their masculine doppelgangers. Maybe they were pushed by abusive fathers or some childhood locker-room humiliation into the business of being tough, or maybe it was true what they said: "Hell, I just wanna lock up Bad Guys." Whatev. I just wanted to hug them, and defrost them by showering some of my special hippie Jew golden love light into their icy blue uniformed worlds.

Neille and I told a few friends, and the more brave of them joined us every other week. One night, one of the cops and I did more than flirt. We connected. His name was Brad and he was beautiful and strong and half-Greek. He was short, as was his last name—Kritt—truncated, he told me, by his father, from the lovely Kritikopolous into something he'd hoped sounded American. Sadly, it just sounded like Crit, as in your backyard critter, such as a garden weasel. I didn't care. We kissed on the dance floor as "Reunited" played on the jukebox. I was Debra Winger, he was my officer and my gentleman.

I gave him my cell number, and every few days after that we would meet somewhere in Hollywood and make out, him being naughty on duty in his uniform, me in my cut-offs and ironic T-shirts he didn't understand. Soon we started trying real dates. We would have dinner, then make out. Go for a walk, then make out. I was fascinated by him. He was fascinated by trying to figure out what the hell I saw in him. He openly said I was amazing and that he was happy to just go along until I got sick of him. This dynamic was new to me, completely different from the big money TV showrunner men I was used to, with whom I'd have to do the Rules for six months, only to win the prize of a relationship where we'd immediately start bickering about things like "tone." Brad and I didn't bicker. We held hands and walked and asked each other questions about our wildly different lives.

Sometimes, Brad would come by after work and sleep over in my apartment on the second floor of a crumbling Victorian. One night, I suggested we spend the night at Brad's place. He gave me his address and directions out to Rancho Cucamonga, a hamlet way east of LA. I packed a demure overnight bag and headed out on the 10 after the Friday afternoon traffic died down.

As I drove I imagined where he lived. It was probably old and woodsy, maybe more a shotgun shack than a house, where overgrown trees would surround a creaky front porch with aluminum deck chairs. Inside, I anticipated a tattered couch, with a crocheted blanket of black and fluorescent yarns, plus wood paneling and a Pabst Blue Ribbon beer sign with a river scene that looked like it was moving.

As I got further out, big, ugly power towers marked the way to nowheresville. Soon the landscape was dotted not with sagebrush, but with big billboards that proclaimed heavenly developments like Royale Estates or Monte Carlo Place. I pulled off at the Rancho Cucamonga exit. There was nothing Rancho-y or Cuca-monga-y about this neighborhood. It was office parks and industrial halogen and lonely strip malls.

When I turned onto Brad's street, I realized I was in the sort of vomitous suburban development of my deepest nightmares. Brad was in his driveway, washing his

big-ass truck, and waved me over. I got out of my car
and gave him a hug. He brought me into his house.

"Would you mind taking your shoes off? I don't like
to get the carpet dirty," he said. Bright track lights illu-
minated white shag, white walls, cream couches, and
hotel art. He proudly brought me past the gigantic TV
and Formica kitchen to his bedroom with his big bed
with that Pillow-Show thing—fifteen pairs of decorative
pillows in descending sizes. That pillow-show shit is one
of my Top Ten Most Hated Things in the World.

"Wow, it's beautiful," I said.

He said he thought maybe we'd go to the store and
get some groceries and cook dinner, then watch a movie.
We were going to do what regular people did. We drove
in his truck to the local grocery store. Our first major
problem occurred in the freezer aisle when he pulled out
a package of toaster strudel and wasn't trying to be
funny. Soon after, he bought barbecue potato chips, calling them our side dish. I kept trying to refocus on his
body and his thick legs and his arms instead of his man-
glings of the English language. I knew exactly how guys
who dated bimbos felt. This was the opposite of regular
life—having sex or making out was fine, while simple,
sober grocery shopping was nerve-wracking.

We made dinner and sat on his couch and watched a
movie on cable. Soon he told me he felt so comfortable
he could confess his deepest secret. I was flattered and
nervous. Had he killed someone? A mortal wound in the
line of duty?

He said he wanted to go into real estate.

"Real estate?" I asked, moving away imperceptibly.

"I want to help people. That's why I became a cop, to try to help people, but it seems like all I do is arrest the same people over and over again and fill out paperwork. I've been realizing lately how much I would love to help first-time home buyers. Do you realize they really get taken advantage of?"

Oh Jesus. My cop didn't even want to be a cop, just an Inland Empire real estate guy. That night, Brad and I had mediocre sex, and fell into dreamless sleep. In the morning, we hugged as if we were human, and I got in my car and drove off, watching the billboards get teensy in my rearview mirror. We were finished and I knew it. The next time he griped that I was too good for him and that it was just a matter of time before I left, I agreed instead of talking him down.

"You're probably right," I said. "It would never work." Brad and I had turned out just like every other relationship—unnaturally high expectations dashed, followed by a door slamming on my soul that said KEEP AWAY FOREVER AND EVER. It always went in this exact pattern—the only difference being whether it took one day or one year to unfold: meet man, like man, dream about man, project a whole lot of things onto the situation that aren't really there, man does something in sex or relationship to mess up projection, never want to see man again.

I guess all of those projections and expectations were a form of objectification. What an annoying discovery: I was the woman who railed against objectification no matter where it appeared. It never occurred to me that it would appear in my very own soul song.

After Brad, I learned my lesson. (Lying.) I continued to gravitate toward the type of man my friends and I called Toolbelts. Toolbelts are construction workers or security dudes, Secret Service agents or firemen. If you're in the film business, they're simply referred to as Below the Line. The line is an actual line on the call sheet or budget. The main difference between these men and your high-class advanced degree guys is that, without being told, they make everything *their* responsibility, from changing light bulbs to basic automobile maintenance to everyone's orgasms.

Remember when as women we were told "your orgasm is YOUR responsibility"? Toolbelts somehow missed that one. Jewish men are prone to stopping halfway through and whining, "What am I doing wrong?" or "Why is this taking so long?" But for Toolbelts, who likely spent their teenage years in a cannery, fifteen minutes of repetitive hand motion is nothing. Even more important, they're responsible for their *own* orgasms. If they experience a momentary erection problem, they simply walk to the kitchen for a glass of juice. A Jewish man is more likely to get teary-eyed, apologize profusely, and raise his arms to the sky to ask, "Why me, God? Why me?"

But as the years progressed, categorizing men into above or below the line, Toolbelt or Palm Pilot, didn't work. In fact, nothing worked. Was it really possible that every last man out there wasn't good enough for me? Rather than contemplate that I might need to make some internal changes, I decided that my problem might be that I didn't belong with a straight man at all. I decided that maybe, what I needed was a gay man.

Yes! The answer to all of my problems! Much like transgender people who felt their whole lives like something was just—off, my soul had actually slipped into the wrong body. Here it was, finally, the truth: I was a gay man trapped in a woman's body! There was so much evidence. I wasn't scared of the cop bar, it felt like heaven to me, whereas a lot of my girlfriends would go there once and never want to go back as long as they lived. I would have had breakfast there if it was a restaurant.

A lot of people, when trying to define homosexuality, point out that a homosexual can sleep with someone of any gender, but only *fall in love* with someone of their same gender. Aha. The closeness I'd felt with my gay male friends was often much closer to love than the negotiations called relationships I'd endured with straight men. I was trapped in a dysmorphic catastrophe. The love of my life would also have to be a gay man. I was going to find a Gay Husband.

I had a lot of gay friends, a few who were even grousing about wanting to give sperm to someone to be a part-time dad. My idea was perfect—my Gay Husband and I would move in together. He'd be the positive male influence in our kid's life. We'd shop together, cook together, laugh at Cheese Nips together. We could share one membership for the Tom of Finland mailing list.

Maybe my inability to settle down was just a homo-y

inclination toward non-monogamy. All those straight men who wanted to own and worship a chaste woman drove me nutso. That just wasn't me, and it never would be. It was hard for me to pretend like I didn't know anything about sex. But with my new Gay Husband, I could be loved for who I was. On Tuesday nights, I'd go out trolling for action while he stayed home with the kids. On Thursday nights, he'd go out trolling for action while I stayed home with the kids. The secret, understood rule would be that no one ever brings the action home, so as not to upset the wholesome homestead that hosted our children's holy home life.

In fact, we wouldn't even have to let everyone know my husband was gay. We'd hold hands in public (sometimes my Gays and I do that anyway), and our sexuality would be private like it used to be in the good old days.

The Gay I wanted most for my husband is my old friend Wayne. He isn't queeny at all, and as an Indiana native, possesses many of the good qualities of El Toolbelt. He's a hard worker and a stand-up guy and you can barely tell by looking at him that he likes to spend his free time face-down in a pillow having his ass pounded by a barely literate teenage Latino boy.

I told my plan to Wayne. He said it sounded good and that, in a few years, if The One didn't turn up, we'd move in together and use a fertility clinic to start a family, possibly even adopting a pudgy Chechnyan orphan just to round things out. I almost hoped I wouldn't find a straight man to spend my life with, as my fantasy of my new life with Wayne sounded better and better each day.

I talked to my psychiatrist, Joy Lowenthal.

"I have an idea," I said. "I'm going to make a life with a gay man! It will be perfect, we'll be best friends and we'll do stuff together and we'll take turns with the chores. There won't be sex to complicate things, so there won't be jealousy or bickering or power plays or tones, just sensational companionship and a two-parent home. Doesn't it sound like perfect love?"

"Not only does it not sound like perfect love," she replied, "it doesn't even sound like love. Or life. Love is messy. Life is complicated. That's what makes it real."

Oh, Joy. Why did she continue to try and shake sense into me? Was she getting paid by the Love Propaganda Board? Was she biased because she had a husband and was trying to get all of her clients to reflect herself in a narcissistic therapeutic miasma? Who the hell was she to believe that little ol' Jill deserved love?

A few months after Brad and I broke up, the Short Stop announced it was closing down. Some LA Westsiders were going to buy it and turn it into a hip bar instead of a cop bar. I wrote a version of this chapter—just the part about the Short Stop, mourning the death of my reverse-gender strip club—and submitted it to the *LA Weekly*. They offered me a hundred dollars as a kill fee. They wanted to do something about the Short Stop's role in the Rampart scandal, as immortalized in *Training Day*, with a sidebar about cop lust, written by someone who wasn't me. When the article came out, I felt proud, even though it wasn't my writing. At least it was my idea. I called Brad. We hadn't talked in months.

"Did you see the article?" I asked.

"No," he answered. "Where?"

"In the *LA Weekly*."

"I don't read that paper," he said. I should have known that. "Did you write it?"

"Not really, " I said. "But you should read it anyway."

Brad and I met up in an Echo Park alley later that evening. He was in his pickup truck, just off duty. I had walked down the hill from my apartment, wearing my ripped cut-offs, with the *LA Weekly* folded under my arm to give to him.

We exchanged pleasantries, did that thing when you ask about new relationships to let each other know you're over it. He had met a nice girl who worked as a dispatcher. I was dating a TV writer. We agreed it was for the best.

"For a while there, Jill, I thought I was in love with you," Brad said.

I smiled. I decided not to tell him that I had thought I was in love with him, too. Instead, I said, "I'm just glad you found someone."

We hugged each other, and kissed one last time for good luck. He got in his truck and drove off. I walked back up the hill. It wasn't until I got home that I noticed I had forgotten to give him the paper.

8

Shoemaker's Daughters

The Shoemaker's Children is one of those ye olde parables about a man who possessed the skill to make comfortable shoes at a reasonable price for the entire village, yet left his own children's feet unshod. Unshoed. Unshod with shoes.

When we were little, my father was an anesthesiologist. But the pressures that went with the job proved too much, and around the time we moved to South Commons he changed his mind and decided he wanted to be a psychiatrist. Finished with putting people to sleep, he now wished to wake people up.

In college and beyond, I met a lot of other psychiatrists' kids, and found we instantly felt kindred. The son of a New York analyst turned me on to the *Shoemaker's Children* theory. Shrink parents are either too busy with their hundreds of other, more important, paying-client brood, obsessed with meta-analyzing everything, or just plain nutty-ass nutbags themselves. So, while children of the folktale walked to school barefoot, enduring the jeers: "Heh heh! Lookit! Ol' Shoemaker's Kids ain't got no shoes!" shrinks' kids go through life as raw, open wounds, little smoke stacks of nerves. "Heh heh! Lookit! Ol' Shrinky's Kid's having sex with a stranger again!"

Do children of the practitioners of the Talking Cure need to act out, perhaps dabbling in the Fucking Cure to get attention? Maybe I did cast my net about in my late teens, twenties, thirties . . . all right, always. But, I didn't see myself as a big ol' skank ho, even though when it came to sex, my motto was, Gotta Try Everybody. I figured, what if you DIDN'T have sex with someone, and he turned out to be The One? And how would you know if he were the one if you didn't have a glance at his psycho-sexual soul song?

I believed in love. I was searching for it, every single day, everywhere I went. But as hard as I tried to find The One, my attempts were hampered by my secret knowledge that I, Jill Soloway, wasn't made for love. I figured I'd never find my soul mate. I'd never have a family, one of those Eileen Fisher extended clan families that take up two pages in a *Vanity Fair* ad, clean cousins and nieces, everyone out on a porch at the family ranch, women with silvery bangs, so many sandals.

Faith and I had it worse than your garden-variety Shoemaker's Children. We were Soloway's children. Less Eileen Fisher, more *Capturing the Friedmans*. I'm not saying there were unspeakable horrors in a basement tutoring program in our house. In fact, I don't even know if there were unspeakable horrors in the basement in the *Capturing the Friedmans* house, because I refuse to see the documentary. All the Jewishness and fondling and first-generation Kaypros are just too damn grody when combined. For my own sanity, I have to pretend it never happened. For similar reasons, I refuse to see *Schindler's List.*

No, The Soloway-Shoemakers Children isn't a parable. It isn't even a story. It's the last line of a story. Fini. Faith and I were clearly meant to be the end of the genetic line. If our family had a two-page fold out ad, it would include a hell of a lot of freaky Jews. We had 'em all: gays, lesbians, bisexuals, asexuals, some of your early versions of transgender. My genetic messaging couldn't have been clearer: No más Soloways. Stop making these people. No one in my generation was getting married, much less having kids. Gatherings dropped off to the occasional funeral. Cousins became e-mail addresses, then unanswered e-mails. My parents divorced, everyone's parents divorced, and the Soloways' genetic future was left in the uteruses of Faith and me: the lesbian and the hoor.

(When I let my mom read this and she got to that line she said, "No, Jilly, don't call yourself a hoor, call yourself a . . . sex enjoyer!" Okay, our genetic future was left in the uteruses of the lesbian and the Sex Enjoyer.)

My sister came out of the closet in her early twenties. But rather than separate us into opposites, it reinforced our sisterhood—neither of us could see ourselves married to a man. It's not like our household was abusive or our family was any more horrifying than anyone else's. It was more like we didn't really have a family. We didn't hang out with relatives or have people over very often. My parents lived in their own world—my mom lost in her diet and exercise obsession, my dad either at work or tending to his depression, a result of growing up in London during the Blitz—plus some unfortunate chemistry. My parents had their own TVs and got together for meals and arguments. There was only one perfect marriage in our home, and it was between me and Faith.

Maybe it wasn't our exclusive, budding-lesbian sisterhood that precluded the idea of finding husbands and making kids of our own once we grew up and out. Maybe we were all just too damn tired. Exhaustion was the most common affliction in our household. My Dad, after crafting psychological shoes for everyone in the village, would come home at the end of each day bushed, calling out: "Oh god, why me?"

He wasn't the only man of his generation whose shoulders slumped with the weight of epochs of anti-Semitism. I don't blame him, but this Jewish despair reigned like a constant humidity in our household, and felt like a toxin to my soul.

Mountains of resentment toward my father began to grow. He certainly didn't see me through his pain, so how could he understand me? By the time I graduated college, the only conversations that didn't escalate into a fight were those about the weather. My sister and I both made our way out into the world, Faith to look for the woman of her dreams, me to fulfill the dream that I'd never have to marry.

Somehow, with the help of luck, the stars, and some scotch tape, my sister and I managed to rise above our tainted lineage and actually reproduce. Faith settled into a Meaningful Lesbian Relationship, and, with a brilliant, handsome vial of sperm, she and her girlfriend had a beautiful daughter. At thirty, I decided I was going to be a single mom. The idea of pledging my life to a man forever was absurd, but I knew that I could promise to love my child forever. That seemed easy. Besides, Jessica Lange and Madonna were having kids without being married, and it seemed really cool. I wanted to be really cool.

I was involved with a man named Chaz when I started feeling the urge to have a kid. Chaz was a WASP from an established Palm Springs family, had numbers after his name, and didn't have to worry about money. Every few months someone would die and he'd have another ten grand to spend. Neither of us had anything going—his dribblings of cash had sapped his motivation to make something of himself, while in my life, the hype from our Brady Bunch play was cashed out and Faith had moved to Boston. I had gotten so good at finding the best pot that I had inadvertently moved into distribution, making a decent living for myself by getting weed for my friends, paying ounce prices and charging them eighth rates. When Chaz and I met at a barbecue, we instantly recognized one another. We were both bored with everything. We went back to my apartment in the middle of the day and didn't leave each other's sides for a year.

Chaz and I were irresponsible together. We were those people who would turn up at your house without notice, ask if we could borrow your tent, open your fridge without asking, pull out a bag of lunch meat, then take off. If you thought you would never see your tent again, you were right. In my wannabe-hippie haze, I told Chaz that now that I was thirty, he should know that if I got pregnant, I would be keeping it. Chaz was fine with that, as long as I knew he was allergic to work and would never be able to support me. Perfect, I thought.

Get pregnant I did. The first few years after our son was born were wonderful. We landed back in the world—we had something to focus on: the most beautiful thing either of us had ever seen in our lives. But soon some instinctual urge toward earning scads of money kicked in. I got motivated. I didn't want my son to go to public school and I didn't want to shop at the Vons, the ghetto grocery store, anymore. Sitting in the food stamps office with the Latina baby-mamas was losing its appeal. I turned into Super Jew and went back to the CAA TV agents I'd alienated after turning into a stoner after *The Real Live Brady Bunch.* I was ready to make some money.

Chaz wasn't. He lived up to his word about never supporting me. When my son was two, we went our separate ways, and I went back into the world to see if my soul mate was someone who was looking for a woman with a son.

Luckily, he was. After I wrote a spec TV script, I got hired on *The Steve Harvey Show* as a staff writer. I slowly worked my way up through the business. In production on TV shows, I had a day-in, day-out supply of toolbelts. But there was an unwritten code among women in the business—sleep below the line, but don't stay overnight there. And certainly don't marry there. But when I got to *Six Feet Under*, the Key Grip put the cops and the Tom of Finland men to shame. He was the manliest man I had ever seen, a man who gave new meaning to the word Moustache, a big man with a little name, Dink. I couldn't stay in my office, I had to see where he was all the time.

I remember calling my mom and telling her I was in love. She corrected me, saying that it was just lust, since I didn't know him yet. She reminded me that I was about to seriously screw things up at the new job I loved.

"What's his name?" my mom asked.

"Dink," I said.

"There's a Dink on every set," she told me. "Go find one somewhere else."

Ah, the ol' "don't shit where you eat" adage. But I've never met anyone who *doesn't* shit where they eat. Everyone shits and eats in the same *building,* their home. Of course you shouldn't sit down for a three-course meal on the floor in front of your toilet. I wasn't planning to make long sweet beautiful love with him in the writer's room, for crying out loud. Where are we supposed to meet people if it's not where we spend all day? What was the big deal?

As usual, I didn't listen. Smart woman, stupid pussy, another writer told me when I informed her of my plans. Dink and I arranged to watch a movie together—as friends, of course. I had entertained the thought that something more could happen. I never imagined that we would fall instantly in love.

But we did. For the first time, that magical chill that runs through your core to let you know He's The One didn't wane after sex. There were no games, no Rules, none of the wave the bunny, hide the bunny games I'd had to play with other men. We simply wanted to do everything together, walk through the world next to each other, every single day.

I didn't know if my utter surety that he was The One was because he was actually my soul mate, or rather, because he was the most absurd possible final choice for a girl raised by exhausted Jewish intellectuals. Dink is nothing like me nor my people. He don't take no shit from no one, and is the most protective man I've ever met. Based on the way he uses his immense power to protect people in supermarkets who get butted in line, I like to believe that if he'd been around, and in love with me, during World War II, he'd have given Hitler himself an ass-whooping he wouldn't have soon forgotten.

Our love surprised me by getting stronger every day. In fact, he's here in every word and page I write—cheering me toward success. It's truly his support that even allows me to write all this. Okay, actually? It's more like the exact opposite of that, to be truthful. It will be a miracle if he doesn't break up with me after reading this. Where he's from, people feel it's rude to ask anything more personal than "Care for some sweet tea?" Every time I've read one of these chapters out loud at a show, our conversation in the car afterwards starts with the same question: "WHY DO YOU ALWAYS HAVE TO TELL EVERYONE EVERY-THING??!!!"

One of the first things I was really excited about—after it was clear our couplehood had a chance—was that my new man came with a brood, a real brood, so unlike the miniature four-legged table the Soloways called a family. When his daughter Natalie announced she was getting married last Christmas, it was time for Dink and me to head down to Alabama to meet everyone.

Tuscaloosa was packed with the three B's: Baptist Churches, Beauty Salons, and Barbecue. Everywhere we went there were those signs with changeable black letters. In LA they say things like "Happy Meals, $1.29." In Tuscaloosa they said, "Christ is the Reason for the Season" and "Canoes and Children are Best when Paddled from Behind."

The people were warm and kind, and I loved the way they unquestioningly gathered with one another every Sunday, the whole dang group at Aunt Susie's. Just to visit. Every Sunday. Same people. Our family had moved to as distant spots as mathematically possible from each other without leaving the country. And all that I considered my extended family were the one-dimensional, five-inch-tall people created by James L. Brooks. These Alabama people knew a secret that had eluded us: Get in the same room with a bunch of people who are kin to you, try not to fight, eat mashed potatoes.

I also finally got to spend time with my boyfriend's daughters. When Dink and I met, Natalie, over the phone, welcomed me into her dad's life with a giant heart, a million-miles-a-minute high-pitched southern accent, and the loudest laugh you've ever heard. Like a sped-up tape recorder, she intoned: "I donno who you are or what you do, I don't care if you're a three-hundred-pound black man, if you make mah Deddy happy, I love you and I cain't wait to meetchyou!"

As a complete aside, I must make mention of the oft-fabled Three Hundred Pound Black Man and his storied sister, the Three Hundred Pound Black Woman. I heard that phrase dropped again last week by a man who felt disappointed his ex-wife wasn't ultimately happy for him after he came out of the closet. He told me: "I would have hoped that after the initial shock wore off, if she TRULY loved me, she would have said, 'I don't care who you're with, be it a dog or a shampoo bottle or a Three Hundred Pound Black Man, as long as you're happy.'"

This wasn't the first time people had waved about these Three Hundred Pound Black people as the ultimate in detestable options. No one in my otherwise liberal landscape would dare pull out just one of those qualities (gayness, blackness, overweightness) and call it unacceptable. But somehow, when combined, they become exponentially unlovable.

Perhaps the world doth protest too much. Maybe choosing as a life partner a Three Hundred Pound Black person of our same gender is the key to happiness. If not, why all the propaganda declaring them the definitive wrong choice?

And what of these people of color who are chubby and gay? Do they have any idea they are held up as a trophy of troublesome blind judgment? Did any overweight, gay black people buy this book? If they did, are they now mad at me? And was that digression worth it? And will it still be here when my editor is done with my book? And what was it I was talking about?

Yes, eldest daughter Natalie pledged to love me even if I was a Three Hundred Pound Black Man, but Amy, Dink's younger daughter by his second wife, was less open to my charms, possibly because at the time I decided Dink was my soul mate, he was not yet legally divorced from her mother.

Turned out Amy was very accepting of me. We all stayed on the same floor in the hotel when we were in Tuscaloosa for the wedding. Amy and I had a lot in common—mostly an unreasonable passion for *The Real World*. One night when we were in her hotel room watching the Paris reunion show, she went off on all the things she hated about her dad. "He doesn't understand me! He doesn't even try! He'll never understand me! He's never even tried!"

Amy taught me something that night, and not just that on *Real World/Road Rules Challenge,* the prize money isn't cash, it's in vouchers. She taught me something about girls and their dads. I knew for a fact that her father loved her like crazy and wanted so badly to understand her. I'd heard him say it over and over again, often to my annoyance if I was trying to read a new *People* magazine. But now that I loved Dink, I had a real window into the dad side, and I was able to see just how futile it felt to reason with the power of teen-girl dad hatred.

I thought up every possible comeback: "You need to let him know you," "Give him a chance," and "I think it's time for you two to have a talk." But nothing worked. When an angry girl wants to blame her dad for every single thing that's ever been wrong in the world, nothing can stop her.

Later that night, from the hotel, this angry Jewish girl decided to call her depressed Jewish dad and just say hi. I hadn't spoken to him in months. The last time he called was to see if the heat wave was as bad as it sounded on TV. As soon as he answered the phone, I said, "I love you, Dad."

"People are flawed, aren't they Jilly?" he asked me. Yes, Dad. People are flawed.

Not a week later, I was back home in LA when I got a call on my cell phone. It was my mom. She said, "Dad's in the hospital."

"Whose dad?" was my first question. Even though her father was dead, I was furjumbled by her calling her ex-husband Dad instead of "your father." It turned out my father had an aneurysm in his aorta and was at Northwestern Hospital awaiting open-heart surgery.

On the plane to Chicago, I cried, less because I was afraid he would die, but more because, ten years after their divorce, my mother was the only person he could think of to call.

When I got to the hospital, my mom had gone home to her new husband. My dad was in a bed in a room on a high floor of Northwestern Hospital, overlooking the lights of the city. Turns out Friday night is a really inconvenient time for surgery, so as soon as they'd discovered in the ER that he wasn't critical, they decided to have him wait over the weekend and get monitored and fluided.

The unit was quiet. He hugged me and cried and thanked me for coming so fast. In his little hospital mini-dress, this giant from my childhood felt smaller than me for the first time ever. A nurse came in to change the tubing on his IV. He was in rare Soloway form, crying out in ear-shattering agony as she ripped tape from his hairy Jewish forearms. All the nurse said in response was a monotone, "he should shave those arms." That night, like a good daughter, I rested his hands over a garbage can and shaved him up to his elbows.

Over the next few days, my mother, sister, and I sat in waiting rooms, most of our focus on who would go to the cafeteria when and get what. I have to compliment Northwestern Hospital's remarkable tuna wraps. Frozen yogurt. Unbelievably good, thick, hot real turkey, green beans, and the most creamery delicious mashed potatoes you'd ever want.

On Monday morning, he had his surgery. One person was allowed to follow his gurney halfway in for a last good-bye. We chose Faith. Or he chose Faith. When she came out she told us that, as an ex-anesthesiologist and a practicing psychiatrist who recognized symptoms of anxiety, he was prescribing himself Ativan down to the final minute. His very last words were a suggestion that perhaps he could tolerate another something milligrams of flubeghshhh . . . and then he was out.

Six hours later, we got word that even though they'd sawed his rib cage open, let a bypass machine pump his blood for him and taken sharp knives to a tiny flap of tissue at the entrance to his aorta, he was doing fine and resting comfortably. Faith and I went into the ICU to see him. He was under, way under, sleeping and wearing a breathing tube and plastic mask. We stood at his bedside, waiting for him to come back from the depths of his anesthesia. We played it like an episode of *Strong Medicine* and he'd been a vegetable for twenty years. We put classical music on the radio and cheered at any sign of life.

As a little time passed, they removed his mask and and his eyes opened like a wet baby chick. That's all he was—eyes, staring out from the prison of his anesthesia. As he came out of it, we decided to help bring him to the surface with a yes and no communication system where he could wiggle his toes to let his needs be known. There we stood, at the end of the bed, each of us holding a bare foot. Here he was, finally . . . the shoemaker. Without any shoes.

My sister and I explained, Dad, your left foot is going to be yes, your right foot is going to be no, okay?

Now, Dad, say yes. Dad wiggled his left foot. We cheered.

Good. Now say No. Dad wiggled his right foot. We cheered.

Left yes, Right No, Good.

"Okay, Dad," I asked, "are you in pain?" But before he could wiggle, Faith said, "I just realized something. I think right should be Yes."

My dad flapped his feet wildly as we meta-analyzed the debate: Faith made the reasonable argument that, as right was the dominant hand, and yes was the dominant answer, right should be yes. I argued that because we had already put the system in place, that was clearly enough reason to continue with it. I finally won my case by reminding her that both yes and left had the short e sound.

Soon after, my dad used his foot signals to make it clear that we should GET THE FUCK OUT. I guess we were annoying him. Oh well. Faith and I took a taxi back to our mom's house, and remembered what it meant to be a Soloway: Pudgy little mouth-breathing tree sloths who watch hours of bad TV, only occasionally gathering the energy to say highly inappropriate things. I knew for sure I was home when, as I lay, half-passed out on the couch watching *Entertainment Tonight*, I heard my sister say in our flat family birdcall: "Mom, do you have any other soap in the house besides the one in the shower because my vagina doesn't like that one."

A couple of days later I went back to LA, and was hit with a renewed understanding of exactly who I am. I'm a mother, I'm a sister, I'm a daughter, but most important, I'm a writer unafraid of literary cliché. No, Gentle Reader, I am not afraid to reintroduce the tedious metaphor you prayed wouldn't find its way back in to end the chapter.

But the metaphor's back. And I'm here to tell you that as we speak, I'm designing my very own shoe. It might be a boot. Yes, in fact, it's a boot, a cute boot, with a Southern flair, and it's worn by the few people in my teeny tiny little brood: me, my son, my husfriend Dink and his daughters, my sister and her lesbian wife and offspring. Yup, we're even approaching something like a clan. There isn't a whole lot yet that we all share, but we do have a few traditions: We watch a fuck of a lot of reality television, say the occasional highly inappropriate comment, eat mashed potatoes till we beg for forgiveness, and rather than walk around barefoot, we make our own goddamn shoes.

9

Black Was Beautiful

Here's that Holocaust chapter I promised you. Sort of. But don't expect much in the way of dates and facts. Most of what I know about the Holocaust I've been able to surmise while trying not to see it but knowing I should, squinting out of the tiniest corner of my eye. I can't look at it straight on, and I can't understand anyone who can. I'm shocked when people drop the word Nazi or Holocaust conversationally in front of my son. Even worse than my fear that he'll ask me how babies are made is the fear that one day he'll turn to me and say, "What's a Nazi?"

How am I supposed to tell him that someone thought it was a good idea to kill six million people just because they were Jewish, like he is? What about the part where everyone just went along with it for a long, long time? What will I say when he asks me why no one could make it stop?

I get mad at those people who offer up other cultures' massacres when the Holocaust is being discussed, à la: "I don't know what Jews are always going on about. What about the Native Americans?" I am sure the Native Americans had it bad, it's just that

(a) changing the subject is an admission of guilt

(b) I'm not Native American.

I also get all incredulous when people say it happened so long ago. It wasn't that long ago. I say it's still happening, for me anyway. Sure, I'm safe and comfy and I have a delightful cup of coffee at my side while I write, with delicious Hazelnut Coffeemate—something that wasn't available during World War II. But when I wonder why I write these words, that beg some unknown "who" to love me, all this tap dancing might be all for him. For Hitler. I sit here tap tap tapping into the night in the hopes that if Hitler could've gotten a chuckle out of something in here, he might have said, "Hold on just one tiny little second, turn those gas chambers off. This is some funny shit. Maybe the Jews aren't so bad after all." I write to find out if all of this distress I have about being too damn sexy is something that he started or that just is. I write to ease the anxiety of hypervigilance. I write to leave something behind, in case he comes to get me.

But I'm barely a Jew. I grew up hardly religious at all. The headline for us was No Christmas. The trendy agnosticism that went with my dad's work as a psychiatrist was the prevailing substitute for belief. No attempt to fill the hole created by the lack of spirituality—just the knowledge that horrible shit happens for no good reason, and it happens even worse to the Jews. There didn't seem to be any reason to proclaim our Jewishness.

When I was five, our family moved to a new neighborhood and stayed there for seven years, until I was twelve. In that neighborhood we didn't think about being or not being Jewish. We thought about not being black.

The development, called South Commons, was on the near south side of Chicago. Built by urban planners in the sixties, between downtown and a no-man's land of projects and railroad tracks, South Commons was a mod collection of brown brick townhouses and apartment complexes, about a square mile around.

South Commons happened way back when the integration movement was starting. The prevailing mood was that in a matter of time, we were all going to love one another and want to live near people of different races. When we moved in, we were part of an inner-city-bound peace march, apologizing for white flight. Idealistic young white families and upwardly mobile black families plunked down what was then the high price of $60,000 to buy narrow, three-story townhouses built in squares around common areas with benches and playgrounds and woodchips if you fell.

Across the street, through gates, but still part of South Commons, there were low-income apartments filled with mostly black families, plus a few Indians and Filipinos with moms who were nurses and dads who were med students at the nearby hospitals. Drawing us together was the dream that all humans needed was the right architecture to get along.

South Commons was definitely not the ghetto, although I keep that quiet when I brag about my childhood. It beats the "my parents were inaccessible" or "I was a dork until I found myself in the drama department" for sheer coolness: "My sister and I were the *only* white kids in the school." I get a gasp of disbelief, then a newfound respect for a few seconds. I'm happy for people to think we lived in a nasty-ass peeling-paint fourth story walk-up, our hair in cornrows, a bag of pork rinds in hand.

I must admit I drew the line at eating pork rinds. I tried one once in the drugstore, one of many attempts in my childhood to make black people like me. But I spit it out when no one was looking. Much like gefilte fish, there's something chemical in certain foods that only works for the group for whom it was created; everyone else gags.

Making black people like me has always been a goal of mine. This annoys black people. I know they shudder when white people act like they're *down*. Some black people hate it when white people use the word "black" instead of African-American. I still don't know what's appropriate, and if someone would tell me I would appreciate it. Some black people hate it when white people capitalize White but forget to capitalize black. More often, in self-hating guilt, I forget to capitalize white but use that big B for Black, just to make sure I don't offend anyone. That all of the b's for black are in lower case, not upper case, was the work of my copy editor, not me.

I really want black people to know I had all the *Color Me Coffee* coloring books as a kid, and that I knew instantly that the Osmonds were a bullshit rip-off of the Jackson Five. I am not like the other white people, I speak their language. When I talk to a black woman, I purse my lips and bob my head ever so slightly, saying "mm hmmm" with emphasis on the "hmmm." If I can wrangle an "I hear you," I am redeemed. If can I get a "*Girl,* you crazy!" I float on air all day. I want them to know that, beneath my Uggs and hundred-dollar vintage T-shirts, there's a chick who's "Young, Gifted, and Black," the song we sang to start our weekly assemblies.

> *Yes, we are Young, Gifted, and Black*
> *and that's a fact!*

Besides singing that I was young, gifted, and black, I also lyrically proclaimed that because I was young, gifted, and black, *my soul's intact,* and, at the song's conclusion, that I was *where it's at*! Of course, this meant that, as a white person, not only was my *soul not* intact, but additionally, wherever I was, was *not* where it's at.

As far as I knew, I was the minority and all over the world, black people were reinforcing their greatness, and all of us low-pigmented, un-gifted whiteys were going to have some serious catching up to do if we were ever going to make it.

In fact, I was more comfortable singing along with the idea that I wasn't "where it's at" than I was mouthing the holiday melodies of Christianity. I devised a system for myself that kept me straight with my Jewish God during caroling season at our school: I decided that I could say Christ and Savior, but never in the same line of a song. That meant that at the end of "Silent Night," I could sing "Christ the (hum) is Born!" or "(Hum) the savior is born!" Even today, as I sing along with Christmas carols, I have to replace certain words to buy Stay-Out-of-Hell points. During the climactic chorus from "O Holy Night," instead of "O Night, Divine!!!" I sing "O Night, So-So!!!" Gotta-be-a-Jew Josh Groban seems to think he's not going to get in trouble for his Christ-loving bellowing, but frankly, I don't know where he gets his chutzpah.

It wasn't until we eventually moved to the near north side in 1977 that I realized growing up in South Commons wasn't normal. After meeting other Jewish kids whose parents were professionals, it became apparent that at some point in our childhood, my parents took a left turn that was very, very different from their contemporaries.

In 1969, my mom was in crisis, trying to make a pretty stack from her prizes won in the Jewish-American Dream contest. My dad was going to be a doctor, after years of my mother working as a teacher to put him through medical school. Back then, instead of getting their MSWs and doing social work like today's Jewish wives, they taught at the inner city public schools.

When my father graduated med school, they bought a house and moved to the suburbs, scrimping and saving to buy one piece of furniture at a time to fill the giant, white-shag-carpeted rooms. They'd escaped the Jewish ghettos of Chicago and made it to this yellow-brick flat house in Glenview, in a subdivision called the Weeping Willows.

The Weeping Willows were filled with people just like my parents, Ruths and Louises and Howards and Barrys, popping out Debbies and Lisas and Jeffreys and Jasons. But while the other moms cooked and cleaned as their children played in sandboxes, my mom actually Wept in the Willows. She sat on the benches with the other moms, wondering how to get in on the recipe conversation without letting it slip that she had no idea how to devil an egg. She soon got wind of the fact that most of them depended on a daily diet pill to get it going and half a Valium to bring it back down. She knew she was about to get swallowed up in a disguise that would eventually suffocate her, and threatened to have a "nervous breakdown" if we didn't move back to the city.

Nervous breakdowns aren't as popular as they used to be. No one has them anymore. Instead people either load up on Zoloft, or, if things get really bad, they suffer from exhaustion and check into Cedars for a little Courtney-Love-esque rest. But in those days, everyone was either having one, or promising to have one, if things didn't change. I imagined what a nervous breakdown might look like, seeing my mom cry, then shake, then throw herself onto the thick, pilly pile of our shag. Surely her cries would turn to screams, she'd vomit, then her nerves would pop out of her flesh, visible like sprung coils on a broken-down Stepford wife. For my mom's sake, I was glad we left the suburbs, although I did feel bad for the friends Faith and I left behind to grow up watching their moms writhe around the floor.

My mom got wind of South Commons in a newspaper article, and wanted to be in on the first wave of the new community. It was within a few blocks of the hospital where my dad worked, so he agreed. It promised the same things the suburbs did: a place where moms could sit around talking while their kids played. Because the houses surrounded the square, moms could even cook dinner while they watched the action out of their kitchen windows. Some would get dinner made and come out to share a glass of wine with each other on their front steps. Husbands would come home, change out of their suits and wash up, and we'd get called in from our adorably integrated games of Kick the Can and Spud. As urban as it was, it truly fulfilled a suburban dream of safe community.

(In fact, now that I'm a parent, I can assuredly say that we all want the exact same thing: a group of kids with whom my kid can play in plain sight, plus a few parents who will sit nearby but allow me to sip a Corona, page through a *People* magazine, and say nothing of consequence.)

Although the square in the middle of our townhouses was integrated, the school Faith and I went to, called South Commons School, slowly got less and less so. In kindergarten, not too long after Martin Had a Dream, our classes were about 50/50. But as the balance changed to 70/30, then 80/20, more and more white families pulled their kids out to go to the private schools of Hyde Park, the next neighborhood south—home to the University of Chicago and a few more whiteys.

No one wanted to be the last white family in the school. Except our parents. When the balance hit 98/2, all that was left was me and Faith. But it coincided with the time when Mom was going to the University of Illinois–Chicago, getting her masters in Urban Planning. Her thesis: integration in South Commons was being threatened by the lack of commitment to the school. She proposed that if parents didn't have all of their kids' common interests to hold the school together, the surrounding neighborhood would fall apart. We couldn't very well leave or we'd wreck her thesis. She was the activist, and my sister and I were her little cardboard signs.

And I had no desire to leave. I felt I fit in fine. It was only when I traveled with my class outside of the school on field trips that I was reminded I was different. On the faces of the crackers of the world who made eye contact with me, I could see they thought I'd gotten lost or had been kidnapped by a rogue band of black children in matching field trip T-shirts. The stupid honkies searched my eyes, needing to know if they should call the police and help me escape.

But I didn't mind. Being the only white girl in my class meant being a star named Gio—that was the way my friends said Jill. Everyone wanted to touch my hair, all the time. If anyone reading this can think of anything that feels better than getting your hair played with by three girls at once, I want to know about it. And I loved their hair too. I'd sit behind Djuana and Wanda, high on

Dark 'n' Lovely, staring at the way their heads were divided into intricate, seven-ponytail patterns, with clear turquoise plastic balls that looked like clickety clacks. The boys' hair was all the same—perfect little round microphone covers. They kept big seventies picks in their back pockets, fluffing at their spongy fro's, all day long.

On share days, a girl named Tanqueray (pronounced Tan*jer*ay) would get up in front of the classroom and sing, better than Whitney Houston in her prime. Cedric would share by doing the Robot or the James Brown, jumping in the air and doing wild pivots with his knees. Me, I didn't share. Not so much.

I got a perverse thrill watching the way they treated each other. "BOY PUT THEM EYEBALLS BACK IN YOUR HEAD!" was a common suggestion from teacher to student. Everyday conversations were chock-full of brutal teasing, kids often accusing one or another of having knees too ashy to leave the house or a mama so fat she finds food in her folds. There was a fight every day, and not just among the boys. One January morning I looked out the window from a spelling test to see two girls ripping off each other's shirts, slapping, bouncing, and dodging in their bras. Somehow, I felt safe, privy to a great seat at the drama, the recipient of a reverse prejudice that worked in my favor.

The more the other white kids left, the tighter Faith and I hung on to our black cred. I easily called white people honkies, laughing at their stiff, dorky ways. Although the black families in the townhouses near us were middle class and were more or less just like us, I preferred spending my time across the way, at the low-rises, where the Real black people lived.

On the way up the stairwell to my friend Takeyah's apartment, the hallways were filled with smells of far away. Early on my nose had a sophisticated, geographically acute awareness of the way soul food came by way of Africa, sniffing out how the greens in apartment 207 mixed with the Ethiopian potatoes from 206, due south of the Indian cumin from 306. The people who didn't have money made up for it by at least having great smells: collards and dirty rice and curry and fried oil. The only delicious aromas of culinary fusion that ever rose in our house were on Saturday nights, when my parents were going out and the apple cobbler accidentally seeped into the fried chicken in our TV dinners.

Over in the delectable-smelling low-rises, so many more people lived together in such smaller spaces. In Damitra's apartment, her grandmother slept on a hospital bed in the kitchen, while four brothers and sisters slept on bunk beds in every room, cousins in the next room, parents on the foldaway in the living room.

Cousins, by the way, didn't have to mean cousins. In early examples of the "it takes a village" method, there was a different way of naming relatives: Kids who had your same mama were your brothers and sisters, even if they were "by" different baby-daddies. No one used the words "step" or "half," ever. If your mother's sister (your aunTEE) had kids, these kids were also your brothers and sisters. Unrelated very good friends, as well as barely re-lated distant relatives—kids by your mama's sister's baby-daddy's other baby-mama—were your cousins. For all intents and purposes, everyone was your cousin.

The unspoken truth was that as cozy as life was on our side of the gate, things could get a little dicey on the other side. Though their lives appeared chock-full of cousins and extremely skilled double-dutch, all of it scored by a Sly and the Family Stone album, problems arose. My sister's skateboard got stolen. There was a rape in a low-rise and a murder in a mid-rise. We started staying a little closer to home, walking a little faster to get to the gates that were now locked, keys distributed to our side only.

My parents weren't ready to move, but they finally decided to send us to another school—a small, private Jewish academy in Hyde Park called Akiba-Schechter. The boys wore rainbow needlepoint yarmulkes and we all davened, bowing at the knees and leaning toward the ark in the chapel every morning. I still had to lip-sync when I sang, but now it was because I didn't have a clue what the heck was going on.

My sister and I also found out we were quite stupid. At the black school we were the smarty-pants white girls. Sometimes I even corrected the teachers. But at Jew school we were the dumb-asses who couldn't even speak Hebrew. Plus they were doing real science with smelly gases and actual dead frogs. There were no dead frogs at South Commons school, no hands-on teaching tools. Instead of stinky, alive formaldehyde, the only smell was cool blue glue heaven emanating from the mimeographs.

Our mom and dad also weren't ready for the new religious demands Akiba-Schechter placed on them. We'd bring handcrafted tinfoil candlesticks home, but my mom would throw them in a drawer rather than put candles in to celebrate Shabbat. Praying and acting Jewish was something our family only did at relatives' houses, twice a year, and that was just as a way to get Grandma Minnie to bring out the sweet-and-sour brisket and matzoh ball soup and potatoes cooked in chicken fat. I guess she was still poor, so she got to have the rich, savory good smells.

On Sukkot, the holiday where you're supposed to make a hut to eat in, my sister and I were under direct orders from Rabbi Rob to build a sukkah with our families. My parents weren't having it. The best Faith and I could do was make construction paper chains and hang them between the recessed balcony railing and the balcony roof. No one ever ate in there, but when Rabbi Rob asked kids to raise their hands if they had a sukkah, we could.

It was also the age when everyone was having bar and bat mitzvahs. We went to a few of them. But no one was thinking about the rite of passage. It was all about sneaking off for make-out sessions. Faith and I got in a fight at one because I made out with Andy Ackerman in the nursery school room. He had told Faith he liked *her* the day before, so he was basically cheating on her with her own sister. Eventually, when the topic of our own bat mitzvahs came up, I had an answer ready: "I would only be doing it for the presents."

This didn't bother my parents. It's not like my father

sat us down and told us there was no God. But I learned from overhearing intellectual debates with his doctor and lawyer friends that they all had the same post-Holocaust point of view: "God? God!? You think a God would let us go through that?"

They have a point. If you're keeping score, it seems a real leap of faith to continue to consider ourselves chosen. Chosen for *what*, some may ask. As for my mom, God was someone you talked to only on days loved ones were flying, as if He sidelined as a temporary travel insurance broker. On weekdays in school, we prayed to the Jewish God. On the weekends and at night, we were atheists who prayed to the god of television. We had started out white, become black, and then were white but Jewish-ish. Our neighborhood was integrated, but our identities were not.

I was also wildly unpopular at our new, tiny school. There were only four other girls in the sixth grade. When I alienated two of them in a typical 12-year-old-allegiance-shifting tribe maneuver, I was friendless. I had one terrific day when Sarah, the alpha of the other four—pulled me into the art room to tell me that I could be her best friend, as long as I didn't tell anyone. I must have accidentally told everyone because a few days later, I was out again.

(All of this was around the time I went to summer camp and was shunned. I'm curious about what it was about me that was such a turnoff. Maybe I was used to being special without having to work at it, and when I got around a bunch of other kids who had been also treated like the messiah by their moms, I had to dig deep to find out what was actually unique about me. Turned out there was nothing.)

We stayed at Jew school for a year as the crime in South Commons got worse. One day I was walking home from a friend's house when a group of low-rise boys swaggered toward me. They were only a few years older, but something in the way they pimp-rolled made me nervous. One pulled his ski mask down over his face, just like that kid in *Fat Albert,* and pushed up against me, brandishing a finger-in-your-pocket gun, saying, "Gimme all your money." The boys were just playing around—they didn't expect me to believe they had a gun, but I was terrified anyway. I ran home and hid in my mother's hug. Everyone's integration dreams were ending.

As we watched the rest of the white families move out, my parents too started to dream about movin' on up, getting a whiff of the coming eighties consumerism. My mom's thesis was turned in and she was exhausted from all that typing on her Selectric and correcting with those little correction sheets you had to stick under the typewriter ball. My father's new psychiatry practice was growing and suddenly we had money to spare. My mom got her first fur coat, a Blackglama mink. We moved to a fancy condo on a beautiful leafy street called North State Parkway, smack in the middle of the Gold Coast. My mom got her second fur coat, an unplucked beaver, a name I wish I had realized how funny it was then as I do now.

In our new life, the only black people were our doormen. Of course, we wanted them to think we were the specialest nicest white people in the building. On holidays my mom wrapped up plates of leftover food with tinfoil to bring down to the lobby. With an overly familiar hug, she'd hand off the gift to whoever was unlucky enough to have to spend his Christmas in a uniform. I felt guilty watching them sit at the Pyrex desk, getting cabs for ladies in heels and hose, heading out into the snowy white night.

Maybe my false black pride is one of the reasons I don't really have any close black friends today. They probably despise me. Or maybe the world just kept turning and landed at a place where for black people, power actually meant admitting they don't want anything to do with us either.

Although growing up as the only white kid didn't make me end up living in a black neighborhood, it did form my most enduring view of myself, that of the Outsider. (I know this must come as a shock to you based on the other chapters in this book.) But to this day, I feel most me when I am in the minority. There is nothing more excruciating to me than the idea of fitting in.

Although I am not very observant, my son goes to a Jewish school. When I first helped myself to a tour of the school on a Saturday afternoon when no one was around, it felt foreign and familiar to me at the same time. I realized it reminded me of Akiba-Schechter—the smell of the kosher kitchen, the cleanliness, the Ben Shahn art in the hallways. Even though I had always imagined my son at one of those agnostic/hippie Montessori schools where no one makes you try, I was suddenly hit with the idea that this was the right school for him. I thought maybe if he could spend his whole childhood there instead of one very awkward puberty year like mine, he might have a shot at something that never felt available to me—a connectedness between his intellect and his heart.

It's not that as a kid and a teen I didn't think—I thought constantly. But none of it was ever put together with school, a place I spent all day nearly every day. I was absolutely 100 percent checked out and faking it, from kindergarten straight through my senior year of college, save for that one women's studies class and a couple of film classes. The fact that I've made anything of myself is a shock to me.

I thought maybe I could give my son the confidence I'd seen on the faces of the kids who spent their lives in private school. I need him to be different from me, not burdened by shape-shifting hunger for identity, for self, for admiration. Maybe these kids had that way about them from being *seen* by highly paid administrators, from having their curiosity endlessly slaked by teachers who weren't angry, starving civil servants.

Beyond giving my son that brain–heart connection I craved, his school is making us less Jewish-ish and more Jewish. They tricked us by starting easy in nursery school, sending home challah and those very same tinfoil candleholders. Next thing I knew, I'd memorized the words to "Hatikvah," looked forward to dancing with the Torahs at Simchah Torah, and made time for Bible study in my week.

I'm happy to let them turn us all into big Jews, but not so that my son will grow up to be super-observant. I do it so that, as they say in certain gospel songs and e-forwarded poems about parenthood, if I keep my feet on the ground, my child can fly. He can rebel against Judaism by considering atheism and Buddhism (but not born-again Christianity). All I need him to know is that he came from a place that is his.

As far as I can tell, he is known at school; he is part of something. When they sing songs in Hebrew, he knows the words, which is a good start. Yet somehow, by being from a nontraditional family—or at least my cobbled-together, single-mom version of a statement about family—I hope I'm sifting in the helpful parts of what I got. Growing up as a minority, for all its problems, at least forced me to look at life through a prism of perspectives.

And maybe, just maybe, he won't be a hypocrite and he'll want a bar mitzvah for the passage instead of the presents. Maybe he'll be able to laugh when he hears the words Chosen People, or put his head and his heart together to find an answer to why Jews always ask, "Why us?" Maybe he'll have an idea of how to replace the self-hating, depressive genes I'm trying so hard not to pass down. Maybe he'll think black is beautiful because he'll never know that anyone ever thought it wasn't. Maybe he'll think Jewish is beautiful. Maybe he'll think his soul's intact, and most important, that he's actually where it's at.

10

Everything Happens for a Reason

Everything happens for a reason.

People say it, yes they do. I say to them, EVERY-
THING? EVERYTHING? Are we *sure* about this one? I
wish I knew what asshole made this up. It's so retroac-
tively faux-helpful, it may as well be Trust Jesus, it's
such a load. It really is. Even intellectuals and atheists
say it; they smile and they raise their eyebrows helpfully,
everything happens for a reason!

But what if nothing happens for a reason? Or if
everything happens for no reason? Or what if some
things shouldn't happen AT ALL?

I sold my house. I am about to move. We have five
days left and my insides feel like a punctured baby pool,
deflating. I live in a storybook house. It's wooden and
small and brown with orangey red undereaves. It's high

on a high, high hill, way at the back of the longest stretch of green green grass anyone ever has seen in Los Angeles East of La Cienega.

I come home from a meeting with a movie executive who listens like a freight train: "UH HUH UH HUH UH HUH UH HUH UH HUH UH HUH" is what she says, a staccato off-kilter rhythm track under everything I say. I hopelessly pitch my ideas at her; they burst into fluffy sad goose eggs, wafting down to the table where she bought me lunch, a lunch to which she was twenty minutes late. I tell her my ideas and she comes at me like a train, UH HUH UH HUH IT SOUNDS MORE LIKE A SERIES THAN A MOVIE WHAT ELSE DO YOU HAVE?

I come home from a meeting like that and open the gate, and I laugh: Look at where I live. I am the luckiest person in the world. My yard is an opera of overwhelming leafy greenness. It's the size of a small park, with this awesome tree smack in the middle of the yard. Shortly after I closed on this house, the first I'd ever bought, I came here by myself and lay down, arms out, part of the grass. I was beneath this giant tree, incredulous at the idea of us. Me and that tree, a hundred or two hundred feet into the sky, fifty feet wide in canopy. That tree was the biggest, tallest boyfriend of my life. I looked up at him and thought, "I love you. I own you." And then I thought, "I could cut you down. I never ever ever would, tree, but I could."

When my son and I moved into this house we were leaving our life with Chaz, leaving the arguments about money and why Chaz had to play electric guitar at two in the morning. Chaz did a lot of passive-aggressive TV watching and made empty promises to get to the dishes. "Yeah, definitely by the time you wake up in the morning. The dishes'll definitely be gone."

The dishes were never done. One night I was heading out to the Mayfair to grocery shop, and I asked Chaz if he could please do the dishes while I was out. I knew he wouldn't, but I said it twice a day anyway. Then, when I was at the grocery store, something happened. I was in the meat aisle and right next to me there was a couple. They had their arms slung around each other, fingers casually stuck in the back pockets of one another's jeans, having a conversation about dinner. Their casual "we've got each other" vibe was identical to the couple on the Costa Rican bus. Amidst a simple conversation, she said something like, "Well, if we do the T-bones, I could make asparagus." And then the guy said, "Okay, how 'bout I make that sauce?" And then the girl said, "Perfect, I'll pick a wine and meet you at checkout." They let go of one another and went off, but I stayed there and felt my eyes well up with tears. I was looking at love.

For all I know that grocery store couple got into a huge fight that night because she didn't let the asparagus boil long enough and he thought the stalks were woody. But it didn't matter. I was done with Chaz. I walked in the door and told him to leave. He did, but for a year after, he walked in without asking, stayed too long once inside. I changed the locks, but we still argued about everything. I knew I had to leave that apartment, because he would always think of it as ours.

When my son and I moved out, and walked into this storybook place with this park-sized yard, we exhaled. It was going to be fine. And it was. It was heaven. While I lived there I found Dink, a real love instead of a tree love. We both fell in love with Dink, my son and I. More than a house, or even a storybook house, this house was a story.

Change is good.

All change? What if someone ran over one of my feet? That would be change. I'd only have one foot. Would that be good? The guy to whom I sold my beautiful little house, David Someone, called to say his real estate agent thought it would be fun if the three of us got together and had a drink. FUN? To listen to them talk about putting a skylight in *my* house? *David, tell Jill what you were thinking—about opening up the ceiling? Tell her your idea about using a giant sharp implement to pry apart her rib cage to stab at her heart. Jill, the waitress is waiting for your order? Are you crying?*

No, I'm not crying, I'll have a mojito I guess.

Leaving my storybook house and buying my new house makes perfect sense. The new house is a really smart buy. The previous owners just fell out of escrow and were desperate to accept any offer so it was really inexpensive. It's on a street where, within one block, two houses have people I know really, really well in them and one has that Rebecca from *Real World* I told you about. My son can stay in the same school, and we can still go to Eatwell, our favorite little diner on Sunday mornings, for pork chops and eggs and gays.

Plus our new house is bigger, much bigger. This storybook house only has room for me and my son, but the new house will be big enough for me and my son and Dink to all live there together, finally, and we need space and it's smart, smart, smart smart smart it's a smart smart move. But I don't want to. I want to stay here in my cute little wooden doll's house.

Let go and let God.

Or let go and let gosh. Either one works because neither one means anything. If you're like me, letting go is easier said than done. My thinking works like a tired kiddie pony ride that goes around the track at Griffith Park for $1.25. Around the neck of that horse is a bucket filled with brain chum. It's not food, it has no value, it's garbage. It shouldn't be examined, it should just be emptied.

But I can't empty it and instead, my mind gets ahold of a problem and goes back and forth over it, around and around the horsie track, until it is understood. Like Bruce Boxleitner. One day I really *saw* the name, truly saw it for the first time and found out it's not Boxelnighter at all, like I'd been saying it in my head. During that week, you may have seen me at in my car, at a red light, moving my lips, Box-leit-ner, box-light-nur, boxel-nighter, over and over again until it was second nature. Boxleitner.

Neuroses protect us from thinking about real things.

That's not an aphorism, that's the voice of Joy Lowenthal, my shrink. She reminds me of things like that and things like, "We worry because we don't want to be present in our lives."

I pay her two hundred dollars an hour, okay, one-twenty-five after Writers Guild insurance co-pay, to tell me that? No, Joy Lowenthal, I worry because I have REAL things to worry about. As soon as we put the offer on the new house, I started worrying. I worried about every single thing, that the bathroom was too close to the stairs and the cost of the renovations and the color of the paint, butternut crème or goldenrod soufflé? Or both on opposing walls? But as the house got ready and the time was coming for us to move, I began to focus all of my worry on the people across the street from the new house.

The people across the street are an elderly Japanese couple, Alvin and Takako, and they're ready in case the Depression happens again. Me, I'm not ready, all my savings are in money, but lucky Alvin and Takako, their savings are in . . . things. Things they keep in their front yard, stuff they could surely barter. For example, after the Armageddon, I wonder what they'd get for that rusty old set of weights holding down the black garbage bags I can see from my new living room. Or the two orange traffic cones, turned black from weather, that you can see from the new kitchen. Or what about the giant, three-foot-tall jar of brown somethings that may or may not be pickled eggs floating in purple water, that you can see from our new bedroom?

Why didn't I notice the people across the street before we decided to buy the new house? Are those things actually pickled eggs? Are they safe for eating after they've been outdoors? In a rainstorm? What are they, really? What are they for? What are they? What are they for? What are they? My brain bucket had to know.

We worry to distract ourselves from our lives . . . because we're afraid of love.

That's Joy again. So I've run out of aphorisms, big deal. And what does my new house have to do with love, anyway? It's just a new house, a bigger house, it's not a story, it's a house where I'm going to live with my son and . . . Dink.

Oh, that's right, this is going to be *our* house. All three of us. Dink is about to give up his apartment because he was never there anymore. And okay, yes, with this new house, he *is* doing everything. He's over there renovating, right now, he's there and he's got a level and he knows how to use it.

Dink told me that, last night while we were sleeping, I woke up, stared him straight in the eyes, and said, "I'm gonna chop you up." Then went back to sleep. I don't believe him.

It's too obvious to just blame fear of love for my obsessions about the panty hose. Have I mentioned the hose yet? Alvin and Takako grow their vegetables in their front yard on strips of old pantyhose. Tomato vines, raspberries, growing on hosiery? And is it hosiery or hoisery? God don't let this be another Box-el-nighter—I mean Boxleitner—I can stop obsessing, I know I can. I promise I'll stop. There's just one more thing my brain has to understand. The octopus.

Alvin and Takako have, perhaps to be neighborly, decorated their rusty front gate with old Christmas ornaments tied on with frayed ribbon. It's June. There's a candy cane ornament and a needlepoint train, a puffy Strawberry Shortcake doll and a snowman from foam balls. And there's the octopus.

One of the ornaments is a yarn octopus. It's a shank of gray yarn with thread around its neck, the splaying yarn separated into eight legs. On the octopus head, there is but one little googly eye, with a long, flirty eyelash on it. I bring this up to Joy, thinking she'll assure me that no normal person would be able to comfortably live across the street from a blind-in-one-eye flirty female octopus.

But Joy smiles and instead tells me that the three of us should make a videotape of ourselves saying good-bye to the old house. We need a ritual, she says. A place to put the feelings.

We did. In the last couple days at the old house we made a good-bye video and we wept and it was good. And on the video if you watch it, you'll see that as I was saying good-bye, good-bye to it all, good-bye to my tree, Dink started to laugh.

"That tree isn't yours," he said.

"Yes it is," I turned off the camera. "I own this tree for three more days, and if I wanted to, before we leave, I *could* chop it down. I wouldn't, but I could."

"No you couldn't," Dink said in his Marlboro man voice. Fuck him and his folksy wisdom and his chuckle that shames me, I thought. "That tree belongs to the land," he continued. "We just happen to be lucky enough to have lived underneath it for a few years."

But that evening, I began to see the house and the tree and the yard as a place that I had been visiting, not a place that was mine. I took my ownership out of the equation, then put the house and the yard and the truth of the move outside of myself, like AA.

We admitted we were powerless, came to believe there was a Power greater than us, made a decision to turn our will and our lives over to the care of God. Or something like that.

There's another tree. This one is in the backyard of the new house. It's a Brazilian pepper tree, with that old old kind of crackling bark. One day I was staring at it, trying to figure out why I didn't like it as much as my tree that was my lover. I finally figured it out. This tree's *bottom* half was that old old crackling bark but the top half was shiny new branches, all much thinner than the bottom half. It looked freaky. Dink explained it to me.

"Someone butchered this tree," he said. I looked closer, and it was clear that in the past couple of years, someone *had* hacked off this tree into naked stumps. At our old house, we'd called in the most expensive tree surgeon to lace it out, shaping and pruning the canopy with loving precision. The people we'd bought the house from had used a saw and a heart of stone. Entire giant perfectly aged gnarled hands from the top of this tree must have fallen with great sound. They probably thought, hey it's our money, we need to do things cheaply, and hell, it's our tree.

"Don't worry," I said to the tree. "While we are here with you, we will protect you. No one will hurt you again."

Ultimately, I guess, it wasn't *letting go* that allowed me to move on. It was anthropomorphizing a thing—that poor tree in the new yard—into something sad that *needed* me to save it. I had to see myself as a special rescue hero to find my way out of the darkness. God, I'm a fucking tool. I really am.

We moved.

I'm writing from my new office. In the old house my computer was in the bedroom, but now that we live here, I wake up before Dink and my son. I come downstairs and get my coffee and pour my thoughts into the computer, in the marine layer morning silence.

And did I tell you about my office? It has purple walls and a hippie-dippie Moroccan bed, and from my desk, I can turn and look out the doors, and I see trees, endless trees, and hills that look like Spain. I don't see the octopus and I don't see the pickled eggs. And there are hummingbirds here. And butterflies. This house, something about it—it seems to attract butterflies. I don't remember ever seeing butterflies at the old house. Change is good.

11

Why Jews Go to the Bathroom with the Door Open

When this book first went to publishers for what became a high-priced bidding war, eventually rising into the low nine figures (lying yet again), the title was *Why Jews Go to the Bathroom with the Door Open.* There are still publishing industry Web sites that announce the sale of my book with that title in it. It really felt like the perfect title to me. I was ready to defend it to the death, to claim it was the only possible right title for my book.

Then I remembered Uncle Sheldon and Aunt Flossy.

My Uncle Sheldon and Aunt Flossy lived in a condo development in the Chicago suburbs. They were the first people who openly proclaimed their right to read while they shat, with signage even. There was a wooden placard on the door that called the room The Library, as well as a magazine rack and a stack of joke books, some with titles like *Bathroom Humor for the Bathroom* and *Two Hundred Best Toilet Jokes.* Here it was, a subcategory of humor—about the bathroom, for the bathroom.

What if people thought my book was a book for reading on the toilet? What if they thought it was a joke book for reading on the toilet? What if they thought it was a joke book chock-full of jokes about toilets?

I couldn't take this chance. I was aiming for the title of The MTV Generation's Susan Sontag, a Fran Lebowitz with Laser Eye Surgery, or An Angrier Natalie Angier. I didn't want to bungle my branding. So when my editor called me to tell me her higher-ups didn't want to narrow my audience by having Jews or bathrooms in the title, I shocked her by replying, "Okay."

"Okay?" she asked. "Seriously?"

I explained to her my reasoning and she agreed. If this book ends up in your bathroom, that's fine, but I don't want it in that section of the Barnes and Noble. It needs to be up front, by the door, on the table with the sign that says FUCKING HILARIOUS WORLD-CHANGING POST-FEMINIST MUSINGS.

We agreed, however, that there would have to be a chapter addressing the question of why Jews go to the bathroom with the door open, because when she was buying the book and my agent was selling the book, everyone wanted to know the answers to the following:

**Why do Jews go to the bathroom with the
door open? and**

Do Jews go to the bathroom with the door
open more than everyone else?

The answer is, I don't know.

I have theories—one about the hypervigilance of
wanting to make sure the Nazis aren't coming again, another about the hyperspazzy need to keep the conversation going no matter what. Or maybe it's just an old,
shtetl-un-fabulous habit left over from the days when
everyone lived in one room anyway, so there was no point
pretending your shit didn't stink.

There are other questions you may be asking, which
I believe I can help you with.

Should you shit with the door open?

Of course not. It stinks. The urge to close the door
on that stuff is instinctual: The vulnerability required to
make a bowel movement is not consistent with a mam-
mal's intrinsic self-protection needs. Hide it, crouch it,
cover it up, keep it from everyone.

But now, the more important question:

Should you pee with the door open?

This still has not been answered to my satisfaction.
When I was a teenager I went with my friend Melissa
to her dad Irv's fancy condo above Water Tower Place.
He had just moved in with his brand-new, twenty years
younger, not-Jewish wife. She was a model and there

were giant photos of just her face, in some cases Warholically doubled and tripled, but without the photo negative effect to make them interesting. She was just—everywhere, her blond-headed head surrounding us in this glass box that overlooked Lake Michigan.

Melissa's father chalked up the success of his new marriage to his latest revelation: "We got separate bathrooms. I've never seen her on the can." Instantly it was clear to me why my parents appeared to hate each other—there was no love because there was no spark because the mystery was gone because they had seen each other on the can.

The Soloway household didn't know from mystery. Bathroom doors were wide open or at least ajar when peeing, unlocked when shitting. There was no knocking, no "excuse me," just a free flow of information, lines of questioning regarding the days' plans or desired lunch choices. Showers and toilets and even tampon insertion were just things that threatened to impede communication. Toilet activities became omnipresent yet ignored, like TV.

Bodily functions were also perfectly acceptable to discuss at all times. I guess it's natural to start talkin' pee-pee and poo-poo when you're raising a toddler. But once toilet training is over, should all reference to these topics cease?

In the Soloway family, there never was such a ceasing. Talk of and familiarity with urinating and defecating continued our entire lives, and still continues now when my parents come to visit or I go home. All of the following are considered acceptable:

Wait here while I pee.

Did you pee?

Did you need to pee before we leave?

Last pees!

Did you have a BM?

Do you need to make a BM?

I need to make a BM, so I'll catch up with you guys at the Olive Garden.

You know what I just realized? I haven't moved my bowels in a couple of days!

Where's Jilly? I think she's moving her bowels.

The newsy status of said movements were just the beginning. Qualitative assessments were also welcomed. My dad was the king of this—Yiddishisms and Britishisms peppered his excited announcements: "Oy, do I have to make a nice scheiss!" or "Not now, I'm sheissing!" And, proudly, placing the *New York Times Magazine* back onto the dining room table: "Say, that was the shite of the month!"

We knew who did what, who had diarrhea, how long it had lasted. We knew who was constipated, who felt constipation coming on, and who was ending a bout with it. Things were constantly being smelled, examined, sniffed, or shared with someone else in the family, often on two fingers held aloft. There was way too much visual and aural overstimulation as well. As a teenager the sound of my dad's pee, particularly the last two or three shakes, was nerve-shattering.

Lonely contemplative afternoons, an hour of meditation, a half hour of musing—none of these things were ever part of our lives at any point. The only person who got any alone time was my father, but less out of respect for his privacy than fear of his bad mood after a long day shrinkin'. My mother, sister, and I were a boundary-less, three-vagina'd lady-monster. Privacy was discouraged, perhaps because it might promote independent thinking and possible disagreement, which our lives had no room for. Faith and I were our mother's right and left leg, and she liked it that way.

To look inward, my sister had the piano as her solace—she would explain her feelings to the black and white keys and fill the house with a beautiful jazzy story. I had nothing, just the ever-returning hug back into my mother's generous bosom. I hovered next to her, head tilted, as she tapped away on her typewriter.

My mother was of no use in helping my sister and me negotiate how much of our bodies belonged to ourselves and how much belonged to the world—it was simple, we belonged to her. I guess that's the way it is at first with all mothers and children. We do what our moms do. Our kids do what we do. My son and I both drink Vitamin Water because I buy it, even though I know it's nothing more than Kool-Aid with smart 'n' jaunty labels. Even if my son preferred, perhaps, Clamato, he wouldn't know it, because he doesn't do his own grocery shopping. He does what I do.

I did what my mom did. As an adult I realize my mom did things differently from some moms. For example, when we were kids, she never taught us you shouldn't sit on toilet seats in public restrooms. Later in life, when beneath the stall wall I saw the straining calf muscles of my neighbor toileteer, I had no idea what was going on. Finally, I saw a friend do it and asked her what the hell she was up to.

"I never sit on toilet seats—they're disgusting!" she replied, displaying an unbelievable talent of concurrently tightening her haunches and loosening her urethra. This was big, big news. I guess she was able to pull off the balance needed for this hovering pose thanks to years of practice. I can't even walk past a yoga studio without falling over, so I promptly dismissed her, and all successive hoverers, as lunatics.

In fact, all of these hoverers who purport to be contributing to decency and cleanliness are actually just disgusting, nasty people. Although I thought I was finished with toilet training when my son was out of diapers, I, at this point, feel called upon to continue toilet training others, specifically, the hoverers, whom I would now like to address directly.

SAY, HOVERERS! Did you know that when you are done hovering, the toilet seat is covered in multi, multi droplets of your piss?

SAY, HOVERERS! Did you know that I have to wipe your piss up with a piece of toilet paper, using my very own hand, a hand that is much better put to use writing humor such as this?

SAY, HOVERERS! At least raise the fucking seat if you need to hover! OR JUST FUCKING STOP HOVERING!

Paper toilet seat covers hold the same mysteries for me as do hoverers, albeit with less bilious rage. I truly don't understand their purpose. As I wept above, a toilet seat with any sign of pee upon it still has to be wiped. Even if you pull your seat cover out of the dispenser, if you are going to use it on a toilet seat a hoverer has marked, you have another thing coming. You still have to wipe the seat off. If you don't, the paper cover will stick to your thighs, using the stranger's urine as glue. The seat covers don't actually save you any humiliation nor contact with other peoples' fluids.

As for their prophylactic uses, there aren't any. As far as I know, women don't slide to, nor fro, nor rub their vaginas mightily on toilet seats. The bodily part exposed to the seat is a stripe on the upper thighs, one on each side. If there was a disease you could catch from the toilet seat, wouldn't my friends have pustules on the backs of their upper thighs? What is it you people fear? Something murkily lurking in the toilet bowl itself that threatens to leap up and enter you, musty secrets from another woman's vagina?

Perhaps a less defensible politeness overlooked by my mother's teachings was that we should wash our hands after using the restroom. I have no idea why my mom forgot to teach us this, but I have crafted my very own reasons around my ways. I feel that if you're going to wash your hands, why not do so *before* you touch your genitals? For those who wash after, might I remind you here that you are not actually touching your ladyflower, but rather, a wad of toilet paper than can easily be bunched thick enough to avoid contact with your own mucousness? And if you do wash after you go, what, exactly, is the point of washing your hands, when there are people like me in the world who don't wash their hands and who touch the door handle on the way out? If you are not willing to open the door with your elbows, you have no reason to wash your hands.

That's correct, you heard me right, if I am alone in the bathroom, I pee, wipe, flush, and head back into Nordstrom. If there is someone else in the bathroom with me, I *will* wash my hands, but only for sound effects purposes. I have even been known to turn the water on and then off again just to allay the worries of my hidden stall-mate, but not actually wash my hands. I only do this sound scam if I am in a hurry, and yes, I do understand that it is pathological.

Now that I have a son, I teach *him* to wash his hands after we use a public restroom. I have been trying to break the generational cycle of grotesqueries which were handed down to me. This is where my deep searching began about how much to see, and how much to let him see. When he was a toddler, naturally, I had to be in the room with him when he went to the bathroom, just to point the manflower, or mayhaps, the manstamen, in the right direction. Now that he's eight, it's probably time for me to start letting him wipe his own ass, but honestly, I really am better at it.

My son has always wanted to be with me when I was in the bathroom. I used to call him my tiny terrorist, like I was a prisoner of war. I would set him up in front of a

Clifford video, then sneak off to the bathroom. The second my legs hit the seat, however, sensors would go off in his brain that would let him know That Lady was missing. Apparently he couldn't stand the thought of me taking a giant crap without him getting a chance to see it all. He'd rush to the door, and start pounding, yelling LET ME IN! LET ME IN! WHAT ARE YOU DOING IN THERE?

I'd cry out in a tragic voice, *I'm going to the bathroom, please let me have some privacy!* His yelling and pounding would stop, but he wouldn't leave. In the silence, I could hear his mouth-breathing panting, his hot red cheek pressed up against the door.

"I know you're out there!" I would cry. *"Please leave me alone!"*

He wouldn't answer. His little breaths would subside and I could hear tiny footsteps walking away. Ahhh. I'd relax onto the can and send signals to my anus that it, too, could relax. But soon enough I would hear his footsteps return, and a book would slide under the door, the teensy tips of his fingers budging it in.

"Can you read this to me?"

"I'M GOING TO THE BATHROOM, CAN YOU PLEASE LEAVE ME ALONE?"

"Yes but can you read that to me when you get out?"

"I WILL READ YOU THE BOOK WHEN I GET OUT NOW PLEASE JUST STEP AWAY FROM THE DOOR. JUST GET AWAY FROM THE DOOR!"

But it was too late. My sphincter had gotten the message: no go. I'd toss my bunched up toilet paper into the toilet, pull up my pants, glance at the empty bowl, flush, neglect to wash my hands, and huff out. "Okay, let's go sit down and read."

I am trying to do everything differently for my son. As a parent, it's my job to protect him from falling down the stairs or eating loads of pixie sticks or sitting on the bathroom floor and watching his mother take a dump every afternoon. Much like pound cake for dinner, just because he thinks he wants it doesn't mean he should.

And now that my son is eight, manners in public restrooms are out of my jurisdiction. We were recently at a movie theater with a co-ed group of second graders when two girls reported that they had SEEN TYLER IN THE LADIES' ROOM WITH HIS MOTHER!!!!!! Powerful peals of laughter erupted that threatened to shake the foundations of the multiplex. The children made a secret, wordless pact to exclude Tyler from all group activities, and it was obvious Tyler would not feel whole again until he got accepted at Wesleyan, a college filled with guys who spent too much time in the women's room.

But what am I supposed to do? Let my precious eight-year-old boy walk into a men's room without me? A room where men STAND IN A ROW AND GET THEIR PENISES OUT IN FRONT OF EACH OTHER?! This is ding dong crazy! What if women walked into the ladies room and there was a row of women sitting on the toilets for all to see? Would we greet each other? Or would we use the same code of silence I hear men use when in the bathroom: Chat at the sinks if need be, but never with penis in hand.

Which reminds me, it's been a few chapters since my political haranguing. The fact that men pee in front of each other and women don't seems to be more evidence of a conspiracy. The world sees male genitalia as acceptable, yet vaginas are so hideous they must always be kept behind doors, stalls, or shrink-wrapped in pantyhose.

And as long as we are on the topic, I guess we should be honest. It doesn't matter how many Women's Studies paintings or self-help videos encourage us to glory in the beauty of our vaginas. I'm sorry, but have you ever just looked down at it and thought WHAT THE FUCK IS THAT? You tilt your head this way, then that, trying to see where the whole 'beautiful' business comes in, but it's elusive.

Returning to my son—which is a really hard thing to do when I'm talking about my vagina—although I've started to let him go to the bathroom by himself, it's not easy. Yesterday after I picked him up from school we stopped at a restaurant in Hollywood for a pre-dinner dinner. After we ordered he said he had to go to the bathroom. I looked around. The place was deserted—there isn't a huge pre-dinner dinner crowd in LA. "Okay," I said, and took a breath. "Go ahead."

I could see the men's room door from where I was sitting and my son headed toward it. But time stopped and turned to slow motion when a man appeared, seemingly dropped from the ceiling. He was potato-shaped, Filipino, and with odd glasses. I say this to give you fun details for your reading pleasure and not to imply that any one or any combination of those three things make someone a child molester. Anyone heading to a deserted men's room with my son—even a three hundred pound black man—would have been suspect. And now Filipino Potato was right next to him, in the middle of the restaurant, heading into the last third of the trek to the bathroom TOGETHER, as together as Karen and Richard Carpenter walking into a sunset on an album cover. I did miniscule calculations that weighed the implied insult against the possibility of a fondle, and my son won.

"One second!" I shouted.

Filitato looked at me. My boy looked at me. "I, uh— wanted to show you this—thing," I said. I looked at the table . . . "in my Dayrunner!" My son came back to the table. I pointed at something in my Dayrunner just in case Potapino was still watching.

"Look, look at this." My kid couldn't figure out what in the world was so interesting about a Dayrunner. In the distance, the door to the men's room closed.

"I just didn't want you to go in the bathroom when anyone else was in there."

He rolled his eyes. Everyone—Dink, his father, his school—had drilled him that he needs to constantly be on the lookout for someone wishing to do wrong things to his privates. When it first came up in preschool, I kept him home the day they showed the cartoony pictures of men with neatly trimmed beards kneeling down to touch the children's crotches. My son hadn't even found out what sex was yet, he hadn't even found out that having a penis was mostly *good* news. All he really knew was that pee came out of it. I needed him to know that his sex organs were primarily there for pleasure and procreation. The idea that strangers wanted to harm him by touching his penis seemed information that needed to wait, at least a couple of years.

Turns out there's no way to win this one. Keep your children home the day they do child molestation prevention and suddenly the rumors flow that you're running a kiddie porn ring out of your living room, and you're off the playdate rotation. It didn't help matters when, after I looked at the literature they were using, I pulled the director of the preschool aside to inform her that they were incorrect in telling the girls that no one should ever touch their vaginas, as vaginas were actually internal sex organs and that the correct terminology was "vulva." Rather than thanking me for the adjustment, she looked at me like I was a nutter.

It was all just too soon and too much, that I knew. I wanted to do it right, this parenting thing. I had to find a way to help my kid grow up without shame about his body. I wished there were a way to make sex be a regular, natural thing, not a frightening, secret thing that only could be cloaked in shame. Luckily, he has made it clear he wants to know NOTHING. Nothing at all. The few times I tried to talk about what sex is, one or both of us ended up crying.

It's not just sex and peeing and bathrooms, I'm trying to get my son's entire childhood right. I look back at mine with such dismay that I question everything I do, all in the name of trying to set up a living environment that won't traumatize him. My parents just went about their business, there was no violence, no cans thrown, and look at me. I've been complaining for 153 pages now and have 75 to go. All I can do is hope that when my kid writes his book it won't be about me.

Early on I decided I wouldn't do anything in front of my child that I wouldn't do on a first date. I didn't want to be in danger of overstimulating him. That meant I couldn't cry, flop around the house braless, or fart, which seemed to be reasonable limits. Soon I took out the part about the bra. If you can't walk around your own house without a bra, what's the point of being home, anyway?

A few years later, when Dink moved in, it was time to incorporate his ways into our family ethos. Dink is one generation older, from The Generation Without Irony. Self-awareness simply is not funny to him. Maybe it's people who remember Kennedy. Maybe it's people who believed in something. All I know is that a lot of people born before 1955 don't like to talk about what they're doing while they're doing it. They don't start sentences with "How weird is it that right now I'm . . ."

This appealed to me in Dink's personality. He would simply go to the bathroom, shut the door, take a shit, and light incense if necessary. Me, I'm not that way. Not so much. I would head toward the bathroom, proud that I wasn't announcing that I was going to the bathroom, pick up a magazine, make a joke on my way in that "just because I have a magazine and I'm heading toward the bathroom doesn't mean I'm going to do anything un-ladylike in there," then shut the door, take a shit, realize

I didn't have matches, run back to the kitchen, yell to everyone to stay away from the bathroom, get the matches, wave them in the air and say, "Please ignore the lady with the matches," run back to the bathroom, light the incense, run back out and try to act like nothing happened, and then comment on the relative success of the entire comedy bit I just did.

Then, as you can see now, it would all get written in a book. But I'm not just writing about what happens in my house when I shit, which would in itself be enough of a problem, but rather, writing about how my examination of shitting continues into writing about shitting, which turns this entire paragraph into the most meta-exhibitionist sense-around logorrheic shitstorm imaginable. In other words, if you aren't running to the bathroom right now to vomit, I commend you.

No, I can't let go of anything, even when it gets ugly, a lot like my mom when she's on a chicken bone. I am first generation Not Jewish Ghetto, but I was raised Jewish Ghetto, which means I witnessed, as part of a daily and regular dinner table show, people smacking and snarking on chicken bones, getting so deeply into the marrow that what's left is a stick of holes through which the wind whistles, people sucking their teeth clean with their tongue and a sharp inhalation, people reaching into their mouth to pick at pieces of beef in a molar. I learned how to crack the cartilage knob off the end of a chicken bone and chomp on it like gum until no more pops are heard, and how to use saliva, even if it reeks of yesterday's red onion, to get stains out of shirts and off of children's faces. I learned that lettuce should be cut by putting an entire leaf into your mouth, using your teeth as a chopper, letting the remainder fall onto your plate. Yes, I saw a lot of things. Bad things.

But now that Dink and I are trying to cobble together our own traditions, I am attempting to weave a tapestry of my overly-self-conscious style with his natural, rootsy ways. Dink instituted the tradition that we close the door when we pee, lock it for anything more. He averted his eyes enough times during meals that he taught me to *cut* the food with a knife before it goes in my mouth, rather than with my teeth, after. He taught me it may not be necessary to get off the phone by saying, "Okay, I have to go take a shit now," and that to leave it at "I'll be going now" is not a sin of omission.

He also taught me that not *everything* has to be hidden, and that it's not just Jews who give bodily functions names. Where he comes from, they call farts "fluffies," which is one of the most disgusting things I have ever heard. Making it sound pink and cute is even worse than referring to it directly. Indeed, he had relatives that used phrases like "wee-wee and dookie," "puddles and bundles," and "sissy and bunches," which made me grateful for something so straightforward as "pee and BM."

To be fair, we do burp in front of each other. Burps are not only tolerated, but welcomed. A particularly resonant one even gets a shout-out, a "nice push" or "lovely" in the call-and-response bird sounds of day-to-day family life. And, if I'm really being honest, my son *does* just freely send farts (I WILL NEVER, EVER SAY

FLUFFY) around the house, as loud and horrid-smelling as anyone could ever wish for, and they are always duly noted.

A milestone in our lives occurred when Dink's teenage daughter visited us and farted loudly in the living room. At first she giggled, embarrassed, and Dink said, "Amy!" But I was trained in the mother-daughter overbonding ways: "Leave her alone," I said, "that's how we know we're family." It truly was a lovely, foul-smelling moment. And hopefully, it's a moment you will find sweet enough to end this chapter. I wanted to craft something delightful, meaningful yet snarky, but if you want me to be honest, and I know you do—right now, like right right right now, my little booty is a' callin' me to run to the can and deliver unto it a big ol' heaping pile of . . . .

I mean, um, I'll be going now.

12

Diamonds

Being a TV writer and producer is really, really fun. As I mentioned earlier, it's like being paid to play a long game of Barbies. There are tons of real-world perks as well: The costume department can get you a Juicy sweat suit wholesale, the set painters will come over and faux wood your fireplace mantle, and the prop girl will let you wear a gigantic diamond ring for a week.

Our prop girl's name was Monica. Any time we had a character who was supposed to be married, she would come to the set carrying a black velvet tray of giant, sparkly wedding rings. In season three, I wrote an episode of *Six Feet Under* that had three suburban wifey types in it. They were waiting in line to see a Dr. Phil–like character we called Dr. Dave. It was the first time I did a superspecial trick in my TV writing: I opened the episode on a billboard of the title of the talk show—*Making Love Work*—which was also the title of the episode—"Making Love Work." I feel the phrase "making love work" is nigh on highlarious because of its double meaning—yes, making love turn out okay, but also making love into a horrendous job, tedious work, which it truly is.

Monica came to me with the tray. All three of these women were supposed to be housewives on their big day out to a TV taping, and so they needed rings, even though there's no chance in hell anyone would see said rings in the final airing. Clearly, the actresses had to have them for their character development. If a character is written as married, they wear rings, even if we never see their hands close up. Now that there's HDTV and Tivo, we do even more detail patrol just to appease the freak who freeze-frames and blows up the picture to catch a mistake and write an angry letter to HBO, demanding a refund from their local cable provider.

All of the rings on Monica's tray were cubic zirconia, but they were the high-end kind that had bands that weren't split on the underside. I chose three for the TV wives, then pulled out one more.

"Monica, could I wear one for a week?" I asked. "I promise I'll give it back to you." She looked around to make sure no one more important than me was watching, then let me take one.

I chose a big huge square cut rock on a white gold band, deciding that it cost around $45,000, and slid it on my ring finger. That day, I marveled at how heavy my left hand felt. Normally I never wear any jewelry at all, neither a ring nor a bracelet nor a watch, so it felt quite strange. I constantly gazed at my $45,000 finger, ashamed at how bad my unmanicured nails looked in such close proximity. One thing was clear—the diamond and manicure industries are clearly interdependent, creating a secret sister-city bond between Cape Town and Phnom Penh that needs to be explored in a documentary one day.

But another thing was even more clear: I was suddenly a member of a club I'd had no idea existed. The scream would start a few feet away and I would tense up, wondering who had fallen off some scaffolding. But there was no fall. The scream was my fault, as Kira from post-production or Gail from makeup was coming toward me. "OOOHHH MY GOOOOOODDDDDDD! YOU FINALLY GOT ONE! AND SUCH A BIIIIG ONE!!!!"

Then they would invariably grasp my hand and wave it about, like the vultures waving Charlie's hand as he held the Golden Ticket, a siren call to all within screeching distance. Women walked toward us, encircling me, each and every one of them needing to see it and hold it up to the light and speculate on its cost, doing miniscule calculations in their miniscule heads about our comparable values.

"OH MY GOD YOU GUYS! JILL GOT ONE! SHE GOT ONE!!!!"

Me, I'm not that way. I see a big diamond on someone's finger and I say in the really high-pitched, legislated, fake way: "Wow! It's really pretty!" But inside, I'm actually thinking BLARGURGH or FLUGHVOMIT or some other sound that I don't know how to spell but it means I want to choke on my own soul.

It's the same sound I make when I see those ads in the *New York Times Magazine* section, the ones that equate diamonds with proof that the woman has been good and deserves something to show for it. There's one running right now that has two diamond rings. Next to the smaller ring, it said "Thank You Honey." Next to the bigger ring it says: "Thank You, God."

That noise, that BLARGRABLLE or JUGHFLUCLT, it used to come up when I worked on my first TV show, with some of those *Harvard Lampoon* guys everyone hears are all over sitcom writing staffs. (They are.) This one khaki-clad, striped-shirt guy, with Kerry hair and a golf course tan, would rock on his heels and say, "Ladies love gems. Don't know why, but it's something I've learned. Ladies just *love* gems." Actually, he said "ladies love Jims," because he was from Texas, and he always chuckled when he said it. But to me, I felt like I was black and he was starting hallway chat with, "Negroes love watermelon!"

He said it so snortingly gigglingly bemused by the fact that when all was said and added up, yeah, sure we won the right to vote and talk and some of us even get paid to use our brains to write comedy like his Harvard fellows, but when it came down to it, all of us could actually be bought off for a pretty rock.

His wife had a huge rock. All kinds of women out

here have huge rocks. Women at the grocery store and the dry cleaners and a whole bunch of the mothers at my son's school, the kind of women who love *Desperate Housewives* and aren't enraged like I am that the women are all too skinny. I know what these women are thinking when they look at me, they think, "Ha ha ha! My man loves me more than her man loves her. Ha, ha, ha!!!"

I knew a wife who got something people in the jewelry industry call a "push gift." These little bracelets and baubles await wives in their husbands' jacket pockets, ready to be handed over after the childbirth moment. Matthew Broderick gave Sarah Jessica Parker a bejeweled charm bracelet in the hospital after she squished their boy James Wilkie out. Good job, honey! Thanks for ripping your pussy open!

I never got a push gift. To be fair, I didn't push, I actually had my son "pulled" through a slice in my belly, so maybe that's the reason. I guess I ate too much and he got too big and he had to be pulled, I didn't keep my weight down, so I deserved nothing, not a diamond, nary a bracelet. When I was laid up in the hospital after my C-section, I couldn't even get anyone to bring me a *National Enquirer*.

Kobe gave his wife a four-million-dollar "I'm sorry I was arrested for allegedly raping someone" diamond. Ben gave J.Lo a billionty dollar pink diamond that still didn't stop her from turning into Runaway Bride a week before the wedding. Pink diamonds instantly made all women with clear—known as white—diamonds ordinary. And now they even have yellow diamonds and *brown* diamonds, called CHOCOLATE DIAMONDS. Can you tell I'm screaming right now? If you're reading this to yourself, you should be screaming anything in all caps in your mind, that's right, scream it loud:

WHAT IS THE FUCKING DEAL WITH THESE DIAMONDS?

I ask you, I really do, WHO ARE THESE WOMEN? AND WHAT ARE THEY DOING FOR THESE DIAMONDS?

Do these women know something I don't know? Are they different than me because their feet look right in a strappy sandal, their toes don't look absurd when painted, like mine do, like donut holes with red dots on them? Do they know exactly what to do when someone slides their chair in for them? Me, I scoot, I'll make a loud scraping noise with my chair, but these women who get diamonds, I bet they glide into the table.

They chew right and they sip right, which is something I don't do. I store my sip of coffee in my cheeks before I swallow it, like a chipmunk. This is something I know I do but I can't stop doing because I don't notice I'm doing it until after I've done it.

These women probably know how to act on dates and how to act after dates. When I was dating it never occurred to me that I shouldn't call the guy the day after and tell him I was thinking about him. No one told me that guys get scared when you pursue them. That's right, no one fucking told me that grown men prefer that grown women behave like bunnies, lifting our little puff tails in the air to expose a millisecond of hole, then scamper off into the forest to incite the chase instinct. NO ONE EVER TOLD ME THAT! I was a go-getter and I figured, why run in the opposite direction when the guy I want is standing right in front of me? Is this why I never got diamonds? I didn't scamper fast enough, or far enough?

I'm serious, I *don't* get it. I ask you, who ARE these women and WHAT are they doing for these diamonds? Do they withhold sex? Have constant sex? Give great blow jobs? Refuse to give blow jobs? Give blow jobs where at first you pretend to not really want to be giving the blow job but then you start to get into it and next thing you know you're just slobbering away like some diamond-deserving secret princess whore of blow jobs? Could somebody please tell me WHAT ARE THESE WOMEN DOING FOR THESE DIAMONDS?

Are they mean? Are they nice? Do they scream? Do they think of themselves as a special prize that deserves special gems? What about special jims? Are their pussies cleaner than mine? Prettier than mine? Waxed? Un-waxed? Waxed with floor wax? Or do they have giant stanky messy hairy retro bushes that don't give a shit at all, bushes that say FUCK YOU, BROTHER, *YOU'RE* GOING TO STICK YOUR FACE IN THIS MESS AND YOU'RE GOING TO GIVE ME DIAMONDS! WHAT IS THE FUCKING DEAL WITH THESE DIAMONDS?

Are they gifts of light for women who agree to be left in the dark? You've been faithful to me for three more years, here's another diamond. You've been raising my children for seven years, your market value has fallen, here's some more diamonds to even it out. Your face is falling because you've been yelling at our children, so you have that line between your eyebrows and sure you'll get money in the settlement but clearly, no one will ever want you again, so Jesus, I hope this rock buys me a few more months of peace in this house, here's another diamond. There's a hole in your soul because you gave up everything for me, is this rock big enough for that hole?

What the fuck are these women doing for these diamonds?

Maybe I'm mad at diamonds because they're a prize for something I'm not good at. I guarantee you if women got diamonds for manic ranting or talking dirty or loud gum smacking, I wouldn't have a problem with diamonds. Fuck the enslaved South African elves or armless children who have to climb down the dirty mines, fuck fashion fascism, de Beers and politics, maybe what bugs me about diamonds is that I'm just not good at getting them.

Maybe . . . maybe you get diamonds for not being angry. Some people say, "Hey, Jill. What's with all the anger?"

It's true, I do, I have rage, I have all kinds of rage about all kinds of things, not just about how no one cares about feminism anymore rage and no one except me wanted to talk about it when Andrea Dworkin died, but in addition, a *what the fuck* rage. This rage is worse in the morning coffee-fueled serotonin rush, where I can be driving to work and on the radio hear 2000 Factory Cash Back on Sienna and I get mad. For no reason. Okay, well, there's clearly a reason there—it should be 2000 Factory Cash Back on *a* Sienna or on *the* Sienna but they just say ON SIENNA like we're all just supposed to intuit that car names don't need articles before them anymore.

And I can't be the only one in this entire universe who became irate upon learning that creamery is not an adjective after all, that it's actually a noun, in fact, a place. Growing up, I had taken all these commercials at face value, believing that rich, creamery butter meant rich, *extra-creamy* butter—butter that's so creamy that it's actually cream*ery.* But then one day I find out it means butter from a creamery, and that, moreover, a creamery is a place where dairy products are made, and I'm not supposed to be angry about all of these years of misleading advertising? I'm not supposed to garner support from everyone I meet on that fateful day of that horrible news, even if it happens to be a first date? Is this why I never got diamonds? Because I never learned how to keep my big, fucking rich, creamery mouth shut?

Sometimes merely the word "Toyotathon" can enrage me.

Or a billboard for the "right-hand ring." This is a new one cooked up by our good friends the diamond people. It says, "The left hand rocks the cradle. The right hand rocks the world." Now, not only am I supposed to feel like shit because my man hasn't spent $50,000 on a ring for me, but also because I'm not willing to spend it on myself? And what about women like me? I like rocking the cradle and the world. Does that mean I need two? I happen to think two would look weird, too symmetrical, like diamond-hand-nipples.

After a few days, I went to find Monica to give her the ring back.

"I thought you said you wanted it for a week," she said.

"I did," I said. "But this thing is really heavy."

I took it off and weighed it in the palm of my hand, then handed it to her. Monica weighed it too.

"I don't know how women wear these things every day," I said. "I just don't."

When I went home that night, Dink said, "Hey, what happened to that ring I gave you?"

"I gave it back," I told him.

"Do you want another one?" he asked.

"I don't know," I said. "Let me think about it."

13

Lesbo Island

Like all relationships, Dink and I came to that place. That moment, when the man you decided was The One does something, a year in or two years in, just as the pheromones are starting to fade. He will toss your child too high in the air while playing in the park or he will tell you he stopped with his friends at Hooters or, in my case with Dink, bring home Hamburger Helper and threaten to make it.

That day will come, and as surely as you felt, He's The One, you will feel, He's Not The One. According to Kabbalah, this is the day your relationship starts. This is the day you become an adult, swallow your pride, and wait it out or work it through.

Or not. If you're like me, you won't swallow your pride. Your rage will start to grow, and you will do what I do—call up Neille and bitch. I start by saying, "Men are obsolete, aren't they? And they don't even know it! None of them are actually supporting us; we're all supporting ourselves these days. The Arrowhead water guy brings my water bottle all the way in to my kitchen if I ask him, and I don't have to let *him* watch football games in the living room all weekend long. And why do men have to answer everything with an answer, even if it's not a question? Or take positions and defend them even when the subject is brunch or which Farmer's Market to try? And why do they look at so much Internet porn?"

What comes next is the invariable plan to start my own society. I go online and look for land in Northern California, and figure out exactly how I'm going to get the fuck out. I make Neille promise to come with me. I make a list of all the women with whom I've discussed this over the years. We tell each other the story of our land particularly during fights with our men, to comfort, using the idea like a suckle toy.

There are a lot of women on that list. First there are all the single moms I know who really could use a village and have promised me they would be on the next plane if I ever do it. Then there are the married women—I know at least ten of them—whose husbands provide financial support in exchange for never being home, being grumpy when they are home, then playing golf on the weekend. They also expect oral sex and tell their haggard, tired wives that a blow job a month is not too much to ask for. But this is where they're wrong. On Lesbo Island, no one has to give any blow jobs. Blow jobs are only given when they're the woman's idea.

That's right, it is now obvious to you that my entire book, as well as my life, has been leading up to this: a call for an unarmed yet mighty revolution, secession into an all-female state, with a big ol' newfounded land, sort of a gigantic honeycomb hideout, ruled by me, yes me, until the patriarchy is toppled and a global matriarchy run by me, yes me, is installed. It's freaky, it doesn't matter if I start out writing about firemen or Tostitos or poodles, everything seems to drift back, like a shopping cart with a broken wheel, to the idea that the only solution to everything wrong with everything is to start a woman-ruled planet, and to begin by starting an all-woman land.

After I get the first couple of girls there, I probably won't tell the rest of the converts that it's forever. This could scare a few women off, women who are probably dominated by their ingrained love of the patriarchy or Blended drinks from Coffee Bean and supermarket sushi. These are the women I would have to trick. To start, I'd just call it "my land," not "our land." I'd also lie and say, "Yes, both of you are welcome. When can you guys come up?"

In fact, to be safe, I wouldn't even call it Lesbo Island, or Wombtown, I'd call it something lovely and lite, like Feather Crest, so people wouldn't have any idea what I was up to. They'd turn up for the nature walks or to sample my slow-roasted meats, perhaps find their muse walking by the blackberry bushes near the pond. But once there, spending their long mornings, magical afternoons, and oh-so-starry nights under my quiet, unspoken rule, they'd start to realize: Now *this* is life. This is how we should all be living. Long weekends would turn into just one more day, until they'd been there a week, then a month.

Frustrated, bored husbands would have long since returned to the cities, like New Jersey husbands doing the shore only on the weekends while the wives kibbitz and sun the rest of the week without them. Back in the city, the husbands would be free to watch football, go to tit bars, and talk about their boring-ass stocks and their boring-ass boring-ass *Consumer Reports.*

Our first Feather Crest Village would be a mock-up for the rest of the lands that other women would make after ours goes really, really well. On about forty acres, we would situate eight or so small cabins, all hidden by enough woodsy goodness that no one could see into your house from their house. This way, any women who like naked stretching can feel free to enjoy naked stretching. I do not like naked stretching, and, as such, nudity will not be encouraged in other parts of Feather Crest. No one should expect to turn up and strut around the pool with their bush on display. That's for inside your cabin.

Every cabin will have its own wood-burning fireplace and kitchen. Women are encouraged to purchase their own groceries and eat in their own homes as often as they wish. In the center of the land, however, would be the (ROUND!) center house—make that Centre Haus—with a giant industrial kitchen, a gathering room (ROUND!) with a fireplace, a gigantic (ROUND!) plasma TV, plus the shed where you keep your blow-up rafts when you don't feel like deflating them for the fall.

At Feather Crest, we'd be the village some say it takes: I could be tap tap tapping on my computer while Lisa hangs out in the vegetable garden with everyone's kids pointing out the difference between arugula and frisee. Later that day, Neille would gather the kids for finger painting while Lisa and I took the station wagon into town for supplies. Every few months, the men would come up for a few days, but as time passed, everyone's relationships would be ruined and instead of visits we'd get checks. If the checks weren't enough, we'd write books or sit in a circle and craft hammocks to sell on the Internet.

It wouldn't have to be hammocks, it could be beaded bracelets or seashell paintings, anything where we sit in a circle and laugh, babies popping on and off of breasts, while through the screened-in porch, we'd watch the older children delight in faerie games. All of that stuff sounds much better than the urban, overscheduled playdate land I live in right now. Right now I only see my women friends every couple months, when we plan a Girls' Night or Ladies Sushi Night. That's right, we actually have to name it to make it happen.

On the land, nothing would be planned. YOU ONLY COME TO THE CENTRE HAUS IF YOU WANT TO. No planned meals, no chore wheels, no meetings, no yoga. If you're at your lil' cabin and you desire some company, you can walk to the Centre Haus to see what's doing, but by no means can you write up a notice saying "Wednesday is Deb's Vegetarian Chili Nite at the Centre!"

As I see it, any sort of planned group gathering is a

recipe for disaster. Nearly all of my daily problems here in the real world are rooted in disdain for plans already made. If I could remove commitments from my life, my mood would improve by at least 13 percent. All my friends seem to feel that way. Most complaints start with "I told Alicia I would be at her birthday gathering but I fucking got my period and I'd give anything not to go." It's the same for my kid. Saturday mornings start with, "Do I really have to go to Jesse's birthday party? Can't we just stay home and watch all those *Wife Swaps* that Tivo is about to erase?"

At Lesbo Island, there are no planned gatherings, only spontaneous ones, so obviously, that rules out E-vites, which I've been trying to find a way to do away with for a long, long time. All of the food would be constantly growing, fresh in the Gardenne outside of the Centre, so if there was a sudden rush of people needing to have, say, an unplanned eighties dance party, there'd be plenty of red chard outside that could be gathered into a basket and boiled into sustenance.

Also at Lesbo Island, as I've implied, there'd be no men as permanent residents, with a few exceptions: anyone's son who was raised there can stay full time until he's eighteen; gay men can visit for up to three weeks a year, though not continuous nor contiguous. Tradesmen from the local town could visit for our ever-lessening sexual needs. Although I've outlawed chore wheels, if the pool of contractors gets shallow, we might need some manner of Cock Wheel on the fridge so no one steps on anyone else's conquests. Ex-husbands—but only those bringing checks—can stay for a long weekend (Thursday thru Sunday or Saturday thru Monday but NEVER Thursday thru Monday); plus any men I say because I'm Queen.

Speaking of which, this is the number one rule on Lesbo Island, and hopefully, in the rest of the world once I'm Queen:

No killing.

This is something men don't understand. They think one has to be able to kill to let eternity know man is here to stay and means it. Super Goddess, the entity to whom we'll pray out at Lesbo Island, knows that the taking of a life is a job for nature only, not man. (Please note that when I write of a respect for life I do not wish to align with pro-lifers or Terry Schaivo supporters.) This idea that life is sacred seems really obvious to me, as obvious as lifting the toilet seat if you're going to hover, but there are millions and millions of men in uniform and in suits who still don't have this one figured out.

Killing is wrong. By the way, it includes Islamic Fundamentalists. Yes, I know a lot of people will tell you Killing is Wrong, but they'll have a little asterisk where they're secretly subconsciously reserving the right to kill Islamic Fundamentalists because Islamic Fundamentalists did The 9/11. But no, in my way of thinking, we can't kill anyone. When I am Ruler of It All, negotiations between nations would start with that awareness, that no man is allowed to take another man's life, even as punishment.

Sure, maybe it's okay if you wanna do other stuff, sure,

cheat on your husband or take the Lord's name in vain, that's all negotiable. I personally love to take the Lord's name in vain; I call out "Jesus on a Cracker!" when I stub my toe.

Also, no one can hurt anyone, unless you're Daphne Merkin and you're visiting and you provide written, informed consent to getting spanked.

Also, it should be clear that although this new land is geared toward exhausted and angry straight women, lesbians are certainly invited, as long as they don't try to start softball teams or build a special shelving unit in the Centre with a sign above it that says, JUST FOR TEAS, PLEASE!

My sister is a lesbian, so she can be there. I don't know whether or not lesbians need to escape from their partners, and if they do, which one will come to Lesbo Isle? That's up to them. I am very lesbian-friendly and only ask that if both sides of a lesbian couple come, they don't fight on the veranda.

When Faith and I were a writing team, people used to say behind our backs, "Which one is the lesbian?" For a while, when I had a crew cut, people thought it was me. But it's never been me, except on a couple of ill-fated attempts to find out once and for all, for sure, for sure, if I was really straight. Nope. Faith has always been the lesbian. Ever since she came out, a lot of people have asked me silly questions about her lesbianishness.

"When did she know she was a lesbian?"

"When did *you* know she was a lesbian?" and, most

important, "Is it possible you made her a lesbian by being so fucking fabulous she loved not only you but all women?" Okay, no one asks me that. That's one I ask only in the privacy of my own bath time.

Faith came out when she was in her early twenties. It was a surprise, yet, as soon as she told me, it put into order everything that had come before it. As kids, when we would go to buy clothes with my mom, my sister would end up in tears. I can still see her looking in the three-sided mirror at Saks, turning this way and that in her gauzy floral dress with sleeves fashioned out of scarves. I don't know what she saw . . . a boy in a dress? A Volkswagen with meat sauce? It was something so incongruous that it made her cry. There were no words, just the familiar feeling of, oh god, Faith can never find anything to wear and now we have to go home early, and I'm pissed because everything looks great on me and I can only buy one outfit.

As I got older, I began to feel more like Faith when it came to dressing like a woman. From fourteen to twenty-one-ish I was happy to don the leggings and miniskirts prescribed by *Seventeen* magazine. After that, I went into worker mode, as a p.a. and documentary film person and then writer. I could wear jeans and funny vintage T-shirts and be just like a boy at work. But now that I'm a woman, it is expected that on certain occasions, I put a dress on. Now, when I stand in the mirror, I feel less like a lady, more like a boy wearing meat sauce or a Volkswagen in a dress. I feel wrong. I want to cry.

Those pointy shoes make me want to cry. Anything

Sarah Jessica Parker ever wore makes me want to cry. Dresses that wrap or are strapless or empire-waisted make me fall to the floor in a crumply pile. When Steve Madden shoes were in I could pull off a heel for a while, finally getting some height, yet staying comfortable, up high on my thick Frankenstein chunky feet. But last year I was going to a meeting and looked down at my Steve Madden mary janes, the top part a brown-on-brown rendition of a schoolgirl shoe, all sitting atop a slightly curvy black brick they called a heel. It was similar to a moment that came a few years previous when I looked down at my miniskirt and said to myself, "This is the last day I'll ever wear a miniskirt." And I was right.

As I stared at my clunky Madden nineties clodhoppers, sadly aware I'd worn them a year or two past their use-by date, something else was clear. Previously I'd never understood how all those old women were still wearing those big bouffant hairdos that took an hour and a half to set, once a week at the beauty salon. But now I realized what was up. These women were still wearing whatever they wore at their primes. I'll stand with this poker hand. No more cards, they said to the fashion world. Because they felt confident for a brief stretch between post-puberty blush and the sags of age, and because this was the moment when they got the most head-turns, they were holding onto it and not letting go, not for their lives, like the way my mom's dog acts when he finds one of her bras on the floor.

Yes, I saw myself at eighty: I'd be stomping over to my Adult Day Health Facility in my thick black-heeled clodhoppers, a miniskirt, ironic T-shirt and long, greasy, flat-ironed gray hair. I'd be like an elderly version of Bratz. Like Geriatz.

That day when I got home I put all my thick-heeled shoes into a bag and threw them up the hole in the ceiling to the attic. One day I'd go up there with my grandchildren, and we would laugh, yes, how we would laugh.

If all of this is sounding good to you right now, tell your girlfriends that, at this new land, there shall be no pointy shoes or strappy stilettos, no pantyhose, no waistbands. I'm not saying it's a place to balloon up and get huge and lose food in your folds and wear muumuus. I do believe bras will still be appreciated, certainly during hikes. But at Feather Crest, we'll get to the business of our lives first and the constriction of appearing womanly somewhere far, far down the list.

When my sister finally did come out of the closet, she did it in a very smart way: She went missing first. That way, when we found her, she could have told us she liked having sex with Danish exercise balls—we were just happy she was alive.

Faith had a boyfriend. She had always had boyfriends. She was no hoor, but at every moment in her young life, there was one very funny cute man who loved her with every fiber of his being, a steadfast, kind partner. I guess when she found a guy with whom she could reasonably pull off the happy breeder charade, she stayed put. At her coming-out moment, she was twenty-three and dating a very funny cute steadfast gentleman named Tim. They had been seeing each other for a few years. One evening Tim called us and said he had been expecting Faith an hour ago, and she never turned up.

Everyone's hearts started beating. This was it. Yes, we Soloways had gotten a pass from God for far too long. Great tragedy—in the form of serial killer victimization—had finally struck. By the next morning the police were on the case and my mom was dashing out an obituary when Faith finally turned up.

Faith had spent the night at a friend's house. And Faith needed to talk to us, my mom said. My mom went first. Then it was my turn. By the time I got to Anne Sather's, a Swedish diner on Belmont that did a really spectacular powdered-sugar-covered crepe, somehow, I already knew what Faith wanted to tell me.

"I think I'm gay," she said. Even then, she knew that the gay guys got all the better stuff than the gay girls. Gay, for one, was so much easier to say, particularly when coming out. Just one quick syllable, over fast, like a shot. "Lesbian" sounds syrupy, like baked cheese, mucous-y. It sounds lazy-bian, like too lazy to put on your pointy shoes and strut your stuff, like you just want to laze into another woman's vagina and forget all the hard work of heterosexuality. Gay, dick. Les-bi-an, va-gi-na. Why the three syllables? Even in breaking away from expected forms of gender roles, the guys got to make theirs gunshot-like—GAY! while the girls' words wave with l's and moist multiple vowels, lugubrious and nubian and malarial.

"I know," I said, as quickly as possible, "and I don't care, you know I don't care, I still love you, of course I still love you, and I'm so sorry about everything horrible thing I've ever said about lesbians, I only said them because you said them too! I really don't care if you want to be a lesbian at all, I love you, Faydo!"

I was apologizing for a lifetime of lesbian-bashing humor that Faith and I started crafting as children. We could have performed a 24-hour set in an anti-lesbian comedy marathon if someone would have thought to invite us. Throughout our lives, we'd made vicious fun of lesbians everywhere we'd seen them—the generous sampling in our extended family, on our high school softball team, and at the gay parade that we found ourselves at every year.

In fact, my main emotion upon learning my sister was a lesbian was to question why in the world she had set me up like that for years—I had only said those things about the one lesbian with the rat-tail haircut, and the other lesbian with the big giant lesbian ass bent over her Hibachi—to entertain Faith—and now here she was, pulling the rug out from under me.

Luckily, Faith assured me that our unrelenting targeting of lesbians would not stop, and that she was the cool kind of lesbian, the kind that was Faith first and a lesbian second, and that we still had all the authority necessary to make jokes about lesbians with too many cats, or who used the word labia too much, or who wanted to secede from men and start their . . . own . . . island . . .

Oh god. Here I am again. It's not that I hate men. I really don't. I'm just mad that I have to walk into bookstores and find a tiny section called Women's Studies. Why can't the men have the tiny section? Why can't most of the books, the books about being human, be written by women? I want to be the syllable (man); I want *them* to be the amended syllable (wo-man). In fact, I'd be just fine to be called Cunt, as long as men could be called Nocunts.

So, sisters, give me time. Keep an eye out for the ads, though they may be a few decades down the road: Feather Crest: We Get It; Feather Crest: 100% Nocunt Free; or Feather Crest: The End of Blow Jobs.

Maybe people will start to take notice of Lesbo Island. Maybe if we build some fences around ourselves so men can't have us they might start to repect us, and then worship us, and finally let us rule the world like we're supposed to. Maybe seceding will make some noise, bring back that resurgence of feminism I keep calling for. There are those two girls who wrote a book about grassroots feminism who have gotten a little attention, but where are the theorists? Where are the Betty Freidans and the Gloria Steinems of our generation? Are we really done making noise?

NO! We will shout from the tops of our roofs at Feather Crest, if we can find the ladders. We will be a model society—not a society of models—getting along without men telling us what to do. We will inspire all of the young flat-ironed *Girls Gone Wild* to let their stomachs pooch out, to be the *Hair Gone Wild* girls, curly and frizzy and free. We will show them that they exist whether or not a man gets turned on watching them lift their halter tops. We will tell them it is probably not empowering to show them your boobs, no matter how many times they tell you to at Mardi Gras. And we will finally be able to ask them, what is that sign you're always doing to show that you love partying, that thing you do when you stick out your pierced tongues? Does it mean "I Love You" in sign language, or "Go Texas Longhorns"? Or "Hang Loose" in Hawaiian? Or "I worship the devil"? And why are you doing it all the time?

No, flat-ironed ladies, at Feather Crest you will let your hair go free and your bushes gone wild. Of course, you need to buy this book, so if you're reading a friend's copy right now, get your own because you'll need it when you apply. You should also probably think *Tiny Ladies in Shiny Pants* is great, supergreat in fact, for it will be our manifesto, actually, our womanifesto, not to be confused with Cuntifesto, a festival we have twice a year with really good barbecue.

If you're interested, please see the back of your book for your application and mail it to me through the publisher. I'm going to go up there and start surveying the land, putting dibs on my cabin site, waiting for you. And hell, if for some reason, my wildly unrealistic expectations are met with thundering disappointment, at the least, I do believe I can get another book out of it.

Appendix 1
or
Brain Pickin's

Even with my mild amount of fame, I've already gotten my share of unwanted attention. Everyone seems to want to know how to get into the business—old friends, friends of friends, relatives I didn't know I had, nephews of women my mom met while naked in the locker room at the East Bank Club, and even my mom. I get e-mails or phone calls, or forwarded messages, all wondering if I wouldn't mind getting together for a few minutes so they could "pick my brain." Don't they realize this hurts? Would they like it if I took a sharp implement to a part of them, just to see what kind of crud I could kick up?

There must be books about getting a job in Hollywood that say: "The key to making it is networking. Contact every person you know, and every person they know who works in the business. Try to arrange something easy like a coffee where you can 'pick their brain.' Every bit of info helps!" Come to think of it, I'd bet there are books that say, "The key to making it is contacting Jill Soloway, 323-555-5763." (Not my real number, do you think I'm an idiot? Yes, that's the old 555 trick!)

And so, I am offering up this chapter with the plan that after the book comes out, when people tell me they'd love to pick my brain about the business, I can tell them that my brain has, in fact, been Fresh-Pict®, and the leavings of it are in the appendices.

1) Write a book. That way, when you make it big, you can direct people to a chapter in your book instead of having lunch with them. Those few cents per book add up.

2) If someone actually lets you see them in person, for god's sake, take them out for sushi.

3) Writers Write. This is something my ex-agent told me when I was bitching to him about not having enough work. He complained about my samples, and I asked him what was fucking wrong with the fucking samples I already had. Perhaps I was having motivation problems because the only variety in my daily diet was bong for breakfast, pipe for lunch, joint for dinner. I harrumphed, then told him, "Well . . . well . . . if writers write, then agents . . . AGE!" Ha ha! I sure showed him.

Sadly, he was right. It wasn't until I actually got excited about writing, real writing, that I had samples worth sharing. Before that, I was only excited about having a big money job in the big money TV business.

It was 1993, just after the *Real Live Brady Bunch,* and Faith and I were in Hollywood, taking meetings as a writing team. As we went on futile meeting after futile meeting, we came up with a new phrase: "Chipmunks in a Tree." We used it as shorthand for "whatever the fuck they want."

It had occurred to us that, as low-level baby-writers, it didn't matter what *we* wanted. Going in with passion projects seemed to be a complete waste of time. It was better to go in, lob shit balls, and then improvise a pitch around whichever shit ball most excited the room. We said in private that we both knew we didn't care what we wrote, as long as we got paid for it—it could even be a sitcom called *Chipmunks in a Tree* about the behind-the-scenes hijinks of people who work on a puppet show called *Chipmunks in a Tree.* Hell, just give us our money.

As much as we laughed and laughed every time we'd sit in a waiting area debating whether or not we should lead or finish with *Chipmunks in a Tree,* we really were way off track. Whether you truly have the passion—which makes it easier—or you have to fake the passion—the one thing you cannot let slip is that you'll do absolutely anything they'd pay you to do.

I liken the TV- and movie-selling world to prostitution. If you ever watch that *Bunny Ranch* show on HBO, which, by the way, should have its own channel because I'd watch it all day long (who signs THOSE releases?!), you'll notice that the women never start out the session with, "Hey, bud, I'm a big whore and I'm just here for the money, so tell me what ya want and I'll do it."

Instead, these chicks actually put on an act like they LOVE sex and they LOVE fat old men in business suits and they're SO TURNED ON that they can't hold back the giggles. Indeed, part of the secret crunchy, baked-in goodness of the john-hoor relationship is that the john enjoys believing the girl really wants sex and likes sex and the money is just a formality. Believing that the whore would be doing it even if there was *no* money is part of the fun, part of what makes this chick a fabulous whore and not his wife. As a writer or producer, you have to have the same conviction—that you LOVE your new show, perhaps called *Chipmunks in a Tree,* and that you think it will not only be hilarious but also revolutionize television.

There's a slightly masochistic part of movie and TV executives and producers that likes to feel at the mercy of the strong-willed egos of the *real* artists. In her book, *The Artist's Way,* Julia Cameron calls these people Shadow Artists—people who in their heart of hearts want to be artists, but don't have the confidence, so they work near artists. She surmises that, as your producers, developments execs, or agents, they have such a love-hate relationship with you that they actually want you to say no—sometimes.

Whether you have the passion or are faking the passion, you should be open to what the exec wants. But not too open. If they want to change it to *Chipmunks in a Chimney,* or *Squirrels in a Tree,* that's just fine. However, if they want *Foxes on a Mountaintop,* get up and storm out of the room, and wait for them to chase you out like a used-car salesman. It's simply part of the deal of working as a writer in Hollywood: Much like prostitution, sometimes people are going to want to pee on you.

If forced to continue the "pitch meeting as sex" metaphor, I would add that as paid sex ends up lacking, you'll always have a better meeting if you're in Real Love. If you wrote what you HAD to write because if you didn't, you would have to be checked into the hospital, if you are compelled to the computer, if the story you want to tell is a story from your very soul instead of a story you think would sell, people in the meeting will fall in love with the project. Their passion will be ignited, which is worth more than decisions they've made with their business sense. When detours arise on the long road to getting your show on the air, or your movie made, your producer's heart fire will sustain the energy, while their initial hard-on might be long gone.

This is why when writers ask me what to do to get started, I quote the long-ago-annoying words of my ex-agent, CAA's Joe Cohen, whose name I won't change like Lotion Bag's, because he'd probably love to see it here. Writers Write. Forget about becoming a writer's assistant, or networking. Just Be a Writer.

Yup, make stuff. Hollywood is chock-full of actors sitting around at the Coffee Bean and Tea Leaf pondering important questions like why that string keeps getting lost in the waistband of their Juicy sweats. There's nothing they want more than YOU, a writer/producer, to look at them and tell them what you see. That's what actors are, empty vessels of wont, giant need babies if you've read your chapters and didn't just flip to the one you thought you could get something out of. Write a one-act play or charge up your video camera and call it a short film. Put an ad in *Backstage* for an open call, and you'll instantly have a couple thousand people standing outside your door the next morning waiting to either blow you, read your lines out loud in front of a camera, or both.

Make stuff. Cast a few people in your play and rehearse it in your living room. Shoot a video and give it a fancy film-look effect on your computer and edit it and show it to your friends. Don't be afraid to figure out what's wrong with it—something surely will be. Don't pay a graphic designer to make a cute cover for it and then wave it around as your first sample—wait. Fix it. Learn from it. Cut it and re-cut it, re-direct it or rewrite it until you've honed your aesthetic, built yourself a voice and a perspective, a vision that you yourself can see. Directing is knowing the difference between what you like and what you don't like. Writing is putting on a piece of paper things you think are either funny or deep.

Sadly, you have to actually do it. Back when I was a weed-sucking, pot-dealing wannabe, I kept hoping that one day someone would come over, knock on my door and say, "Jill, let's see what's hiding in that My Documents folder!" No one ever did.

4) Write a short story or an essay. As I said, a lot of the TV writers I know only want to write that hot sample to get hired—this year it's *Desperate Housewives* or *Lost*. And yes, you need it. But you should also have all

kinds of other stuff, and again, not just stuff you wrote to get a job. Everything recent and good in my career happened because of *Courtney Cox's Asshole,* the short story I mentioned in the first chapter. I wrote out of frustration at not having heard my own comedic voice in so long. I wrote it for myself and to make my friend Becky laugh, and we started a reading series so I'd have somewhere to watch her perform it. The original spark of it was that small, the spark of the absurd humor between best friends. But after hearing the audience laugh, I got up the nerve to send it to the literary magazine *Zyzzyva,* where it eventually got published.

The feeling of seeing your stuff in print, in a font other than Times New Roman, is a buzz. Be it an essay or fiction, it truly is a great first step in feeling like a writer. Literary magazines actually *do* read anonymous submissions. There is no way sending your script blindly to a studio will ever get it used as anything more than a door stop, but by putting stamps on manila envelopes and mailing things off to lit mags, you will get responses and if you're any good, some of your stuff will actually get published. Again, you must actually print the stuff up and put it in the mailbox. These magazines do not have the budget to send people to your house, knock on your door, and ask you to show them everything you've written.

You can find lists of the good ones in *Best American Short Stories* and *Best American Essays,* which come out every year. In the back, there's a list, with street addresses even, of the places where they get their stuff. If you can't get anything published in a literary magazine, at the very least get it published online. If you can't get published online, you probably should consider being an agent. To find out how to become an agent, I suggest you take one to lunch and ask if you can pick their brain. One we like: Joe Cohen at CAA.

The other important thing to know is that I wasn't sitting around blowing bongs when I wrote Cox's A. The stoney baloney part was six years earlier, before I had a kid. When I wrote the fabled anus tale, I was working as a sitcom writer. And when I got that sitcom job, it was because of a sketch job I'd gotten from someone who was familiar with me from *Real Live Brady Bunch.* In other words, there's no such thing as a Cinderella story when it comes to writing. And in other, other words, in fact, so important it should get a number,

5) STOP SMOKING POT. I'm serious. Just stop it. I know it's the best feeling in the world, and if you're self-medicating so you don't kill yourself, then fine, keep smoking because I certainly don't want your blood on my hands. But it's the biggest motivation killer in the world and if you're a guy it gives you man-breasts and it doesn't make you a better writer, it only makes you *think* you're a better writer.

6) Brand yourself. As a writer, unlike an actor, you don't have a face—just a name. From the moment you start writing, even in film school, you must brand yourself. I've met quite a few young writers who have a pen name and then, their real name. Often times both are on the front pages of their scripts. It will say the title, followed

by: by Fiona Rockenwagner. Then at the bottom there'll be a contact name and phone number for someone named Fiona Leigh Schmidt, or even worse, Karen Schmidt.

This is really bad and superconfusing. If you have more than one name, all of your potential word-of-mouth is cut in half because half the time people will be talking about you using the name they call you, while the other half the people will use your stupid nom de plume. Do you think The Cheesecake Factory would enjoy the enormous success it does if every other week, it changed its sign to That Pie Emporium? Just pick your fucking name and get over it. No one wants to know which is your birth name and what's your pen name. Besides, pen names make you look like a freak. And,yes, I once did a mailing of submissions under the name Sophia Soleveichik. Sometimes we think we have to change our names to give ourselves permission to write, but this is just the fear and self-loathing that goes hand-in-hand with being a writer. Recognize that fear as the uninvited guest at all of your parties, and move on.

Also, registering your stuff with the Writers Guild and then putting that information on your script makes you look like a paranoid freak. It's a complete waste of time. Nothing belongs to anyone. The definitions of "Zeitgeist" and "meme" are proof that everything belongs to everyone. Many, many people have the exact same ideas at the same time. In fact, I wouldn't be surprised if more than one person came up with the idea to name the concept Zeitgeist at the same time. Last year, word has it, there were hundreds of spec screenplays about guys rescuing adorable strippers, many of them single moms with initials like CJ or AJ.

Most of the time these matching ideas will spontaneously self-generate. Millions of us watch the same television programs, and millions of us can add. Ideas are just things we've seen, adding or subtracting other things. Only on the incredibly rare occasion will people outright steal something they overheard at the next table at Swingers. Do yourself a favor and forget about all of this ownership crap. Unless you're really litigious and like trying to find parking downtown near the courts, there's no point in trying to protect your writing. Build a career, brand yourself, write every day, and no one will be able to steal anything you write because your voice will be something only you can do.

7) No one, including me, gives a shit about your ideas. I get e-mails and phone calls from people who think that coming up with an *idea* is the ticket out of their tedious life as a hairdresser in Iowa City. WRONG. No one buys ideas from people who aren't in the business. If they do I've never heard of it. There are two kinds of producers out here, non-writing producers and writing producers. Non-writing producers get paid for their experience. Writing producers get paid for their voice. If you can't write, you need experience, so get out here and start at the craft service table like the rest of us. This entertainment business is an industry, not a lottery. We all had to work. When you think you can jump in without doing the work, it's an insult. Would you like me to come to your beauty salon

and ask if I can do just one person's hairdo because I had a great idea for a style?

8) Everything everyone says is a lie. When Faith and I first got to town while producing *The Real Live Brady Bunch,* the people at Paramount requested a meeting with us. We dressed like professional ladies and went to meet a very important movie executive who shall remain nameless but if you worked at Paramount during the mid-nineties he was the one who looked like an alcoholic marionette. He had a cute young development girl with a name like Pheefo.

They effusively told us that they had *us,* only *us* to thank for revitalizing the *Brady Bunch* brand name, and that they were so grateful we raised so much interest anew in their show that they wanted to involve us on the ground level in a movie they were going to make. In fact, they wanted us to write the movie, and probably even direct it. I mentioned that we had never directed a movie before, but the marionette told us he was sure we could handle it, as the Director of Photography does all the work anyway. We hugged everyone good-bye and walked out of the meeting, and when we were far enough away, we did that side-kick-heel-click thing. When we got in the car and closed the doors, we screamed, little tears in our eyes, fumbling for the phone to call someone, breathing those unbelievable soul sighs that say, "I made it!"

We never heard from Paramount again. We never even knew for sure that we weren't hearing from them again. This thing happened called the soft pass. It's a way of being rude that involves a slow recession from the scene of the crime. At no time does the executive turn and run in the other direction and scream NO! I DON'T WANT YOU ANYMORE! They just walk backwards, smiling, moving ever so slowly, until they're in another state or a different year. Calls are returned during the other person's lunch break. To salvage self-respect, agents then double the amount of time it took to get their call returned before they call. Before you know it, you've "fallen off" the other person's phone sheet. This is something people really say: "Oh my god! I'm so sorry we never connected! You must have fallen off my phone sheet!"

You can tell you're getting a soft pass any time your agent reports back to you that he and the exec are "trading," which means trading calls, which means they're hanging out in the hallways talking to their colleagues about whether or not they find Teri Hatcher's protruding clavicle attractive. There's a whole other language agents speak that takes a while to learn: "I left word" means "they hate you." "They're interested" and "they're very interested" means "they hate you." "They love you" and "they love the writing" means "they hate the project." "They love it but they have to talk to Carolyn" means "they hate it and they want to put the blame on someone else, just in case you ever do anything worth wanting."

Similar to the "soft pass" are the "glass plans." These are either social or business plans, made where both parties are fully aware they'll never actually be kept. They are a way of saying, "later!" but involve the use of assistants' precious time to keep a charade alive, scheduling and rescheduling lunch, then breakfast, then cocktails, then a conference call, until someone drops off the other person's phone sheet, and a miniature version of the less powerful person is crouching under the more powerful person's desk, geschrying in a teensy voice, paralyzed from the fall.

9) Everyone thinks you suck until you don't. It takes one great person to say you're great before anyone else will. Mine was Alan Ball. Before he liked me everyone else thought I was just okay, that I had potential. People do this—wait for someone bigger to jump on board—so that if I write something so horrible that a test audience says, "This reeks of ass!" whoever hired me can shrug and say, "Alan Ball liked her."

It is possible that by the time this book comes out, a movie I have written will be in production, or even in a theater near you. Just last week, regarding a screenplay I wrote called *Tricycle,* they threw around the names George Clooney and Jennifer Aniston as the leads, and before that Brad Pitt and Kate Winslet. Luckily, I know enough not to do that silly side-kick-heel-click when I leave the office anymore, and in fact, not even to tell anyone. Except all of you.

Getting movies made is like this gigantic energy roller coaster, with ever-increasing tries up the hill until there's enough power to go over. The interest of people who have track records of making large amounts of money informs the velocity. If Julia Roberts loved it, the coaster goes higher. If Soderbergh's office is "just trading," the ride slows down. It continues like this, up, down, more people jumping on or off to be near the perceived hit or non-hit, continuing until the release of the movie.

And if you think TV is like a big ol' Barbies game, you ain't seen nothing. Movie producers are eight-year-old girls sitting on the floor playing dolls, even if they're Harvey Weinstein. Which two haven't we smashed together yet? I wanna see my Drew Barrymore doll on top of my Clive Owen doll! No, put the Ashton doll on the Reese doll! Hey, I know! Let's take off the Angelina doll's pants and make the Brad doll kiss her ladyflower!

Not that I know anything about movies, or getting movies made. I've never had one made. I overheard a dinner party conversation some development girls were having, placing writers in one of two groups, either "he knows what a movie is" or "she has no idea what a movie is." Frighteningly, there was also "he used to know what a movie is but he forgot." I have no idea whether or not I know what a movie is. I should know, because I've been to a few of them, but until one that I've written opens and opens big, I can't be sure.

10) You know that feeling? That sigh of "I made it!" that my sister and I mistakenly had in the parking lot of Paramount? It never, ever comes. Never. Every moment when you're supposed to be feeling that apex of joy, perhaps at the Emmys or Golden Globes—you feel nothing. Just sadness, really. Most people I know bring a half a Vicodin or something to get through it.

11) Oh, on second thought, smoke all the pot you want. Who am I kidding? There were many years when marijuana was the only thing that made me want to write. But after watching countless friends fight with sobriety, and wondering when and how I would ever be able to stop smoking pot, I now believe that the only solution for addiction is to make your life something for which you want to show up. The main reason I can't be high anymore is that I'm doing something I want to get right. But I'm not here to judge. Do what you have to do. Just make sure you take at least one sober pass at whatever you do before you turn it in.

Appendix 2
or
More Pickin'

And now, the answers to the most frequently asked questions about being a TV and movie writer.

1. On *Six Feet Under,* does each of you write for a different character? Yup, that's what we do, we all jump around in leotards and improvise in character, voices and all. Nooooo, I'm lying. We don't do that. We each write our own scripts. We give each other feedback and help each other outline, but we write from the privacy of our own hells.

2. Why are there so many producers? There aren't really. There are just a lot of titles that writers can have and a lot of them have the word "producer" in them. The titles go in a very specific order, just like the patches you get as you move up the ranks in swimming at camp. These are the titles, and each year, you move up one, bringing with it a slight increase in salary:

staff writer—tadpole

story editor—minnow

executive story editor—executive minnow

coproducer—koi

producer—trout

supervising producer—supervising trout

co-executive producer—whale

executive producer—whale shark

3. **Will you read my screenplay and give me feedback?** No. Will you come over this weekend and give me four hours of your time? You could re-sod my yard, actually. No? I didn't think so.

4. **How much do TV writers make?** Two thousand dollars a week. This is the starting salary for a staff writer and it doesn't increase until you become an executive producer. It works like this: as a staff writer, you get Writers Guild minimum, which was around $2,000 a week when I started. Your agent feels so bad for you that you have to live on that amount of money in LA that he doesn't take his standard 10 percent commission. In year two, you make 10 percent more, so your agent takes out his commission and you're back where you started. In year three, you start wondering why you're not making any money, and have lunch with a guy who says that as your manager, he can make more for you, so you agree to try it for a year. He gets 15 percent. You figure if you've lived on two grand a week for two years, you can do it again.

By year four you really want them to demand more money for you. Your manager tells you it's illegal for

agents and managers to negotiate—they're only allowed
to take you to lunch and call you on Saturday mornings
to see if you want to meet them at the mall with their
kids. By the way, don't feel bad that I'm making fun of
agents. They're the last remaining group it's PC to make
jokes about. Remember when John Lennon said Woman
is the Nigger of the World? Agent is the Nigger of the
Hollywood.

What you really need is a lawyer, so you finally find
a lawyer whose connections and cojones can get you a 5
percent raise. But when the lawyer gives you his bill, you
say you can't possibly afford that, and he says fine, I'll
just take 5 percent.

The next year there's a reality TV boom and half as
many written shows, so your agent tells you everyone's
dropping a level or two just to work. You go back down
to executive minnow. Then, a couple of years later, someone says *"Desperate Housewives* killed reality!" and you're
back up again. Now your gross income is over $200,000
a year and you can't stand to see what's being taken out
for taxes. Besides, everyone says you really should incorporate after that amount, and all your friends have cute
names for their corporations like Monkeys R Us Inc. and
All Girls All Day Productions and you get jealous. You
want to incorporate. You get high and make a list of
twenty cute names, or you dig through your files and
find that list of band names you and your friends made
when you were high, and you pick one.

Now you need a business manager who can register
this name with the state for you. He charges 5 percent

and so although you're making scads of money on paper, you're still only seeing about two grand a week. Finally, the next year, you've got some breathing room. Whew.

But you realize now that you're incorporated, what you've been getting lately are *gross* checks, and a ginormous tax bill is due. Your business manager puts aside the money and doesn't let you touch it unless you want to go to jail with Martha Stewart. You're back to just under two grand a week.

I've heard that when you become a showrunner, which means you created the show and it's airing, you get extra money. Every time the show airs you get checks just for having been there when it was created, also known as Malibu money. I want Malibu money. I want that black American Express Card that Britney's brother pulled out to pay for lunch when I met him last week to discuss projects. Also, Jessica Simpson has one. She even loses hers.

That's not so much to ask, is it? A black American Express card, and maybe the chance to fly in a private jet with Sean Penn and talk about scripts, once before I die. And three $10,000 vacations a year. And a pool. Just a little pool. A teensey, tiny pool, like half spa, half pool. They call them spools out here. I'll take just one.

Appendix 3
or
Oh, Yeah

Yes, I want to be in charge of everything. I'm completely spazzy and I won't be able to calm down until I start my own land, incite feminist revolution, you know the drill. But if I can't do that, I have a few more things I really, really want to say, because if this doesn't sell more than 15,000 copies, these people are never going to let me write a book again. Lemme lay 'em on ya:

1) **THE FOOD COURT TRAY RULE.** People, from now on, no one gets a table until you have your food. It's that simple. The current system is clearly discriminatory against single people. Just because YOU have a lunch date who can go grab the table while you go up to the counter and order the Chinese chicken salads means you can eat sitting down while I stand there holding my tray like the fat tuba player in the high school lunchroom? No. Not anymore.

2) **E-DRESS.** Isn't it a great word? Take it, use it, spread it, hell, copyright it for all I care. Isn't it much more fun to say than "What's your e-mail address?" Wouldn't you rather say "What's your e-dress?"

3) **NO FREQUENT ANYTHING CARDS.** They shalt be illegal. No Coffee Bean cards that get punched each day nor frequent Barnes and Noble cards. Carrying a fraying card for fifteen weeks is simply not worth $3.85. Especially because you always lose the thing with one punch to go. Also, no airline mileage programs. Airline tickets don't cost that much, nowhere near as much as the time spent trying to track down your miles and get them rolled over from the previous year. Get rid of them. Too much work. Never worth it. That's what I say.

4) **SINGLE LINES AT MULTIPLE ATMS.** Even at ATMs where they don't have a painted line on the sidewalk, it's up to YOU to start the line. If you are the first one in line when there are patrons at more than one ATM, please, be responsible and stand in THE MIDDLE of all the potential lines. Encourage others to stand behind you. If you see them playing their luck and picking a favorite, loudly say, "One line!"

5) **STOP THE EXPLOITATION OF SAND-WICHES.** Please, folks, no more of those giant-sub-sandwich mascots waving at cars in front of the Subway sandwich shop. In New York, I think you guys have waving hot dogs. It seems really hot in there. I can't help searching the netting for the humiliated eyes, like a woman in a burka. If they keep it up, we should stop buying our sandwiches there, no matter how low they

pretend their trans fat grams are. Similarly, the job where someone has to stand holding a plastic arrow pointing toward a new apartment complex, waving it up and down ten thousand times in one day, is wrong.

6) **GET THE FUCK OUT OF THE WAY.** If you are coming through the gate at the airport and you see your loved one, please MOVE OFF to the side for your hug and embrace and face-squeezing "Oh my god, Cody is so big!" The rest of us are trying to get through. Also, friends, as you head onto the escalator, if you would like to stand, please do so on the right so that the rest of us might pass.

7) **I KNOW THE REAL REASON MUSLIMS AND JEWS DON'T GET ALONG.** I didn't have room for this in my introduction when I discussed how religion divided women into chaste vs. whore as a tool to separate us from our power. But there's yet another supersecret thing that I never hear anyone talk about.

To reduce a Bible passage to its most basic, and sorry, God, if I mangle it: Abraham was married to Sarah but she couldn't beget him a kid, so she asked her personal assistant, Hagar, to sleep with her husband and make a baby for them. This is as bad an idea today as it was back then. Abraham not only enjoyed the sex with Hagar, but also had warm feelings toward her offspring, Ishmael. Then, Sarah got lucky and begat Isaac. But Ishmael's teenage ways got on Sarah's nerves. So Sarah sent Hagar and Ishmael into the desert to die. Isaac married Rebecca and they started breeding lots and lots of nearsighted Jews. Meanwhile, back in the desert, not only did Ishmael have the gall to NOT die, he actually started his own religion, Islam, and started breeding Muslims. That's right—it is possible that all of the hatred between Muslims and Jews is a simple case of one family of kids hating Dad's mistress's kids. Underneath this current conflict that might end up blowing up the entire planet is the old Madonna–whore triangle, and the question of who Dad loved more. We hate them because their mom had an affair with our dad. They hate us back because our mom called their mom a whore. Dad didn't follow *their* mom into the desert to save her. I can kind of see why they're pissed. If he didn't want to be with her, the least he could have done was make child support arrangements beyond bread and water. Interestingly, in the Muslim version of events, Hagar is the beloved wife and Sarah is the tainted concubine. Either way, there's that triangle that polarizes women again.

8) YOUNG LADIES, PLEASE STOP LETTING WHITE BOYS CALL THEMSELVES PIMPS. What's this "pimp" thing all those young guys are always going on about? Do any of these college girls who giggle know what a pimp is? Yes, a pimp wears a fine fancy hat and gets all the ladeez, which is admirable. But real pimps have four or five women who suck stranger's dicks and then give their pimps 100 percent of the money or get the shit beaten out of them. That's right, 100 percent. Is this as big news for you as it was for me? I figured most pimps took a 50 percent cut. It seemed only fair. But the industry standard is that the ho only gets the semen she's swallowed and whatever apartment and clothes the pimp lets her keep.

Please, friends, stop these guys from even joshingly referring to themselves as Pimps, be it in their e-dress (à la CoolPmpn@pimpville.com), in the way they "pimp" their rides by putting dubs on the wheels, or at the Pimp N' Ho parties they host at their fraternities.

9) **IF YOU DON'T WANT ME TO BE THE AN-TICHRIST,** use condoms. I don't mean to yell at you. I thought I would be writing comedy essays. But my editor told me to write whatever I wanted. Oh, poor, poor Free Press. I pulled one over on them. This is what all of this adds up to: I'm just that lady who tours the country with a slide projector and a bag full of plastic cervix models, a campaigning, annoying, cajoling hygiene teacher.

Women are in a really precarious position, maybe because we are born with a limited number of potential ovulations and men are born with more sperm than there are grains of sand on the globe times a bajillion. Let that help you realize, young ladies, that you are guarding a precious resource—your future children. Men don't have a precious resource; their sperm is a dime a bajillion.

I got my period when I was seventeen (another story, I know) and may enter menopause at, let's say, forty-nine. With twelve periods a year, that's 384 potential babes. Not so many when you think about it. It would be a lot of kids if I had to give birth to all of them, but, as chances throughout your life to make a child, decreasing each month as you ovulate, they are pretty special.

This might account for the diamonds. This could be the reason some women think of themselves as special gems, or even special jims—they are the guardian of 384 potential humans on this planet. Men can't have children without them.

I know why people think family is the future. I know why Dr. Laura acts the way she does. I know why society gives promiscuous women a hard time. Because if all women waited for a big diamond ring and a promise of fidelity before they let men at their 384 sparkling, golden magic beans, things could be a lot easier and safer. It might increase the chance every child would have two parents. It would be nice if every child had two parents.

It might be nice. It could be nice. We have no idea because asking women to make men wait is a fairy tale, not reality. Reality is that many women have the urge to have sex just as much as some men do. Reality is that nobody realizes how precious their 384 are, like when we let somebody take us on a motorcycle ride, we don't realize how precious this one life is. Reality is that if any of this sex-positive-feminist stuff is actually going to work, and if I'm going to leave all of you flat-ironed porno girls alone because all you're doing is wearing the fashion, and who am I to stop fashion, you have to promise me one thing.

Use condoms. They were invented by humans who were invented by god, so they're here for a reason, and everything happens for a reason. Condoms are the universe's way of saying it's okay to have sex without the rock. But you actually have to use them. It is no more likely a guy is going to open your purse to look for condoms than it is that the editor of *The New Yorker* was going to come to my house and look for pithy stories. In fact, the guys are more likely to say, over and over again: I don't like condoms. I hate condoms. Condoms feel like taking a shower with a Ziploc bag on my head. Let me just put it in for a second. How about just a minute. Maybe just the head. I'll pull out. I promise. I'm really good at pulling out.

They're really bad at pulling out. The idea of not being allowed to come inside you excites them so much they come inside you. Then, they get up, towel off, then go downstairs to see who won the game.

Now you have their semen inside you. Let's say you're their partner and you want to get pregnant. This is the only instance in which still having their semen inside you is a good idea. For everyone else, all the time, it is a HORRIBLE IDEA. The worst idea you can think of.

When I was a teenager, it was a bad idea because you could get pregnant and you would have to get an abortion. Enough people got enough abortions under comfortable enough twilight sleep that getting another abortion was even a fair enough risk to take the next time a guy said "Let me just put it in for a second" and you didn't want to be a dork and bring out a condom, or, even worse, argue and see how far they would push it.

But now it's worse for so many reasons. Now there's AIDS. A woman having sex with an HIV-positive man is *seventy* times more likely to contract the virus than a man having sex with a woman who is HIV positive. It's obvious why. While the man is emptied of his fluids and is downstairs watching the halftime show, we're lying around up-stairs, a petri dish in our vaginas. Our internal sex organs are like an actual ooey, gooey medium. They've got the kind of sticky stuff going that scientists try to create when they want to see if they can make a virus grow. As the receptive partners, not only do we receive, but we also cultivate and breed, and not just humans.

Besides AIDS, there's an epidemic right now called HPV. Turns out every single one of those dreaded abnormal Pap smears that we ever got were caused by a virus that was carried in some guy's sperm. HPV is spreading like wildfire and if left untreated, it evolves into cervical cancer. It's treatable, but the treatment involves literally slicing off the very ends of our cervixes, or possibly, cervices. After a few of these treatments, your cervix is shorter than it should be, so it can be hard to hold a pregnancy. This is also treatable, but none of this stuff bodes well.

All of it implies that it doesn't matter how sex-positive we get as feminists—lots of sex with strangers or even good friends is not necessarily all that positive for our bodies and particularly, our 384. But this doesn't mean women should be less familiar with sex. My solution is not to put women into burkas or white doily out-fits or set up societal shame or cut off their clits. My solution is to know. To have knowledge and share knowl-edge and speak and write books and learn everything we can about our bodies.

Young women, listen to me: We have to know how to consent. We have to know how to make those pimps put on condoms or walk away if they don't. We have to not be afraid of how it looks to behave as if we know a lot about sex. We cannot be so drunk and high when we do have sex that we can't remember to use condoms. We can't be so ashamed of wanting sex that we have to get drunk or high to have sex.

We have to feel like special prizes and treat our bodies like sacred flowers. And if, like some women, we employ the fantasy of having sex without our consent, we have to have a nice, dorky conversation about it first and make sure a condom is used. We cannot get drunk and just see what happens, then tell all our friends we were date-raped. There is such a thing as real date rape, when women take drugs they don't know are hidden in their drink. There is such a thing as real rape, when women are alone and surprised in the night. Using the word "rape" to describe sex that happens when we're too drunk to remember it is an appalling insult to the women who have had to endure real rape. What really did happen in the room between Kobe and the young woman? Who knows. But know that we rape ourselves when we give up the ability to meaningfully consent. Camille Paglia was right when she said men cannot be trusted. Most of them can't. Know that.

We cannot, instead of asking for sex because it seems too wanton, just put ourselves in situations where sex happens. Particularly as high school and college women, but truly for all women, we must know for sure that what is happening is something we wanted to happen.

And if some of you want French manicures and to

wear jeans where I can see the outline of your labia and that baby prostitute perfume and nipple piercings and you want to go to Cancún and make that devil party sign and show them your boobs, have at it. Just know what you want, know what you've had to drink, and remember that even though your whole life you have been told it's your job to say no, it's also okay if you say yes. And if you say yes, do so with your eyes open.

Don't be the girl at the top of the telephone pole. Yes, they just want to see your panties. Come down from that pole, return the gaze, and make sure you have a condom in your Hello Kitty purse.

10) **MY WOMEN'S STUDIES PROFESSOR WAS RIGHT.** Yet again, I forgot that lesbians had feelings too, as evidenced by my sperm-specific sermonizing in number 9. All I can say is, I'm sorry.

11) **HELP ME, WON'T YOU?** I can't do this alone. I know a lot of women have written books but there's still a lot of catching up to do, if we're ever going to get back to the sacred 50/50 balance intended when God or whatever made both of us, man and woman. So get started.

APPLICATION TO LIVE ON FEATHER CREST

Name: _____

Address: _____

City, State, Zip: _____

Phone: _____

Alternate Address (where you can be reached if you and
    your partner get in a fight) _____

How much money will you donate to the Feather Crest
    Foundation upon moving in? _____

How many children do you have? _____

Are they well behaved? _____

When they hit puberty, will they be willing to babysit the
    younguns? _____

If you have a boy, is he aware he will be chased into the
    woods when he turns eighteen? _____

Have you ever been in a cult? _____

Are you susceptible to cults? _____

Do you have anything against cults? _____

Name five women friends to whom we can send applica-
    tions. Our movement is growing and word of mouth is
    our favorite advertising! _____

✂

Hobbies you are willing to share with the other women by heading a workshop (circle all that apply):

beading	knitting	veggie growing	HPV treatment
handiwork	needlepoint	herb growing	midwifery
journaling	crewelwork	weed growing	sushi chef
improv	lanyards	cooking	web site mainte
poetry	god's eyes	cleaning	nance
macrame	Web site	Pap smears	guitar
	design		high-pitched
			folksinging

Are you a complainer? Circle one: not so much / so much / a fuck of a lot

Have you ever been kicked out of a group? Please describe when/where. _____

Are you willing to throw away your flat iron? _____

Are you one of those people who say you get along better with men than with women? _____

Do you plan on blogging from Feather Crest? _____

Are you willing to let the entire thing be (a) filmed as a reality series or will you (b) huff off, accusing me of only pretending to care about women but secretly, I'm a publicity whore who only wants to profit from everything and be on TV once and for all? (Circle one)

Acknowledgments

Huge amounts of thanking go to: my mother, Elaine Soloway, who told me I should have every little thing my heart desired and then taught me how to write so I could explain it to everyone. My sister and best friend, Faith Soloway, whose laugh has always been and will always be my most coveted reward. My father, Harry Soloway, who has the driest and best sense of humor ever, who is a great father, a great psychiatrist, and a brilliant man, and has quite the generous spirit for not taking anything in here too seriously. He has also asked me to let everyone know that he *wanted* me to come home early from camp and was *not* listening to the Cubs game during the conversation with the camp director.

To Amy Scheibe, my brilliant editor and friend, who told me to write whatever my little heart desired—just like my mom. She inspired, coaxed out, and shaped all of what is here. To Maris Kreizman, who is amazing and who helped Amy help me; to Martha Levin and Dominick Anfuso, for their thoughtful guidance and confidence in me.

Thanks also go to my book agent, Dan Greenberg, who plucked me from online obscurity and told me he liked my writing and thought I could sell a book, to Hilary Carlip for putting my essay on her site in the first place for Dan to read, and to Amy Sohn for telling Dan to go find me.

To the Tiny Ladies ladies: Carol de Onís and Kathryn Higuchi for the fabulous copyediting, Heidi Slan, Jennifer Shoucair, Michele Jacob, Carisa Hays, and Suzanne Donahue for their work on publicity and sales, and Jennifer Weidman for all things legal.

To Alan Rautbort, who has loved me and believed in me since the beginning.

To the audiences of *Sit 'n' Spin* for listening and laughing and being there as much of this material developed.

To the other people who read early drafts and gave me their valued feedback as friends and editors: Sandi Wisenberg, Susie Bright, Harlyn Aizely, Neille Olson, Tom Madison, Bonnie MacFarlane, Ellen Silverstein, Becky Thyre, Cara diPaolo, Brett Paesel, Sarah Thyre, Lisa Kimmel, Anne Preven, Bernie Boscoe, Mary Wachtel, Jenifer Potts, Maggie Rowe, Jaclyn Lafer, Rabbi Michelle Missaghieh, Rabbi Lisa Edwards, and Jonathan Ames.

Large, large thank yous to the other writers at *Six Feet Under,* my sweet friends who had to listen to me rant and rage about things as I was working them out in my mind for this book. They also all read drafts of it and gave me great feedback: Alan Ball, Craig Wright, Kate Robin, Scott Buck, Nancy Oliver, Rick Cleveland, and Bruce Eric Kaplan.

To Jen Braeden, also known as Jennie Loughridge and Jane Braeden, for being in my head with me at all times, helping me with every single thing, and to Jasmin Segura for being in my house at all times, helping me with every single thing.

To my other Hollywood peeps: again with the Alan Rautbort, Patty Detroit, John Huddle, Howard Altman, and Karl Austen, who manage my career and sell me about town in the most caring and respectful of ways.

To Claudia Lonow, for inventing the phrase "Pornoization of America" and sharing it with me in the bathroom at Rob Cohen's party at the El Rey.

To the Mothras, for being the people who populate the little performance space/nightclub where I hear my voice in my head. The Mothras who haven't been thanked in other sections of this thankfulness: Amanda Lasher, Cynthia Sweeney, Erin Hosier, Holiday Reinhorn, Jessica Kaminsky, Justine Bateman, Lisa Carver, Missie Noel, Paula Killen, and Shana Berger.

To my friends and some other people who have encouraged my writing or told me I could write or provided inspiration for what is in here: Eric Waddell, Madeline Moskowitz, Ron Zimmerman, Carrie Aizley, Melanie Hutsell, Tom Rogers, Mike Waterkotte, Rino Liberatore, Ron Lazzeretti, Angela Brown, Nonnie

Brown, Oona Beauchard, Jonathan Schneidman, Sarah Silverman, Mick Napier, Mark Platt, Alan Poul, Joanna Lovinger, Christina Jokanavich, Ally Brecker-Shearmur, Terry Sweeney, Lanier Laney, John Levenstein, Peter Hems, Howard Junker, Abby Wolf-Weiss, and Robin Ruzan.

To my sorta-step-daughters Amy and Natalie for giving me so much love for being their Other Mother, and,

To my partner Dink for being so easy to love, for loving me, and for making a life with me that is beautiful. And to my son, for being everything.

About the Author

Jill Soloway was a writer on *Six Feet Under* for four seasons, most recently as Co-Executive Producer. She joined the staff for the second season after working on TV shows including *The Oblongs, Baby Blues,* and *Nikki.*

She started out doing theater with her sister Faith in Chicago, where they created the generation-defining stage phenomenon *The Real Live Brady Bunch* at The Annoyance Theater. That play eventually went to the Village Gate in NY, the Geffen in LA, and toured the country and the world. She and her sister also created, directed, and performed in hit plays *The Miss Vagina Pageant* and *Not Without My Nipples.* With Maggie Rowe, Jill produced a night of comedic monologues and music called *Sit 'n' Spin* in LA, as well as *Hollywood Hell House,* a straight-on walk-through performance of the actual haunted houses the Christian right uses as a conversion tool.

About the Author

Jill's first short story was called *Courteney Cox's Asshole*, which was published in *Zyzzyva*, then subsequently in *Best American Erotica 2003*. Jill has also written a novella called *Jodi K*, which can be found in Susie Bright's collection, *Three Kinds of Asking For It*. Jill wrote many pieces for the *Six Feet Under* book, *Better Living Through Death*. This is Jill's first real, whole book that's just her.